*1. Paschal Mystery*

# THE PASCHAL MYSTERY
# AND CHRISTIAN LIVING

# THE
# PASCHAL MYSTERY
# AND
# CHRISTIAN LIVING

### Very Rev. James Alberione
### S.S.P., S.T.D.

*Translated by the Daughters of St. Paul*

Our Lady Queen of Peace Books
and Mission, Inc.
4920 22nd Avenue
Brookings, SD 57006
605-693-3983

NIHIL OBSTAT:
 Rev. Edward Douglas, S.J.
  *Diocesan Censor Deputatus*

IMPRIMATUR:
 Richard Cardinal Cushing
  *Archbishop of Boston*

ISBN 0-8198-0114-3 cloth
ISBN 0-8198-0115-1 paper

Library of Congress *Catalog* Card Number: 68-28102

Printed in the U.S.A. by the Daughters of St. Paul
50 St. Paul's Ave., Boston, Ma. 02130

The Daughters of St. Paul are an international congregation of
religious women serving the Church with the communications
media.

# Contents

# INTRODUCTION

The Paschal Mystery, center and heart of Christian life, is the mystery of Christ, Who achieved His task of redeeming mankind and of giving perfect glory to God principally by His blessed passion, resurrection from the dead and glorious ascension.

In a series of considerations permeated with a profound and sublime spirituality, the well-known author presents the Paschal Mystery in the light of scriptural texts, deriving therefrom practical applications which urge us on to enter into the mystery and make it our own.

"Christ Jesus," says St. Paul, "humbled himself, becoming obedient to death, even to death on a cross. Therefore God also has exalted him" (Phil 2:8-9). We learn from the same Apostle that we must always bear about in our body the dying of Jesus, so that the life also of Jesus may be made manifest in our bodily frame (cf. 2 Cor. 4:10).

Father Alberione invites us to thus make the Paschal Mystery relevant in our lives and reproduce its reality in our hearts, identifying ourselves with Christ, so that baptized into the death of Christ—"united with him in the likeness of his death, we shall be so in the likeness of his resurrection also" (Rom. 6:5).

Important and timely, deeply spiritual and inspirational, *The Paschal Mystery and Christian Living* makes rewarding reading for religious as well as laity, and is most useful to the priest as a source for homilies. All will find this book truly valuable as a stimulus to spiritual growth and holiness.

# The Passion
of Christ
in Our Life

They were now on their way, going up to Jerusalem; and Jesus was walking on in front of them, and they were in dismay, and those who followed were afraid. And again taking the Twelve, he began to tell them what would happen to him, saying, "Behold, we are going up to Jerusalem, and the Son of Man will be betrayed to the chief priests and the Scribes; and they will mock him, and spit upon him, and scourge him, and put him to death; and on the third day he will rise again."

And they understood none of these things and this saying was hidden from them, neither did they get to know the things that were being said.                Mt. 20:17-19; Mk. 10:32-34; Lk. 18:31-34

"If we are sons, we are heirs also: heirs indeed of God and joint heirs with Christ, provided, however, we suffer with him that we may also be glorified with him" (Rom. 8:17).

The days of life pass; the Christian should progress in love of God, in virtue and in merit. A great means to this end is meditation on the sufferings of the crucified Savior, since, as the Church reminds us in the *Apostolic Constitution on Fast and Abstinence:* "The task of bearing in his body and soul the death of the Lord affects the whole life of the baptized person at every instant and in every aspect."

When St. Philip Benizi lay on his deathbed, his strength almost exhausted, he asked his religious: "Bring me my book!"

The brothers looked at one another perplexed. Then one brought him the breviary, one the missal, and another a book of meditations. But St. Philip shook his head.

Someone then handed him a crucifix, which the saint brought to his lips and kissed with joy. "This is my book," he exclaimed: "the crucifix!"

Many are the mysteries to be penetrated in meditating upon this book. The first of them is always this: the Son of God loved us so greatly that He laid down His life for each one of us, as the *Constitution on the Church in the Modern World* phrases it: "As an innocent lamb He merited for us life by the free shedding of His own blood. In Him God reconciled us to Himself and among ourselves; from bondage to the devil and sin He delivered us, so that each one of us can say with the Apostle: The Son of God loved me and gave Himself up for me (Gal. 2:20)."

The crucifix should intensify our love. It should also stir up our sorrow, since our sins are responsible for Christ's passion and death.

And then, the crucifix should inspire our confidence. Jesus has merited all for us. Faith in Him, united to good works, will save us.

Meditation on the crucifix produces repentance, sorrow and conversion. All of these are necessary for the following of Christ—all are relevant to the Christian of today. In the *Apostolic Constitution on Fast and Abstinence*, Pope Paul VI declares: "We should like today to repeat to our sons the words spoken by Peter in his first speech after Pentecost: 'Repent...then for the forgiveness of your sins.' And at the same time we want to repeat once more to all the nations of the earth the invitation of Paul to the Gentiles of Lystra: 'Turn... to the living God.'"


On one occasion, when Philip Neri's exhortations failed to move one of his penitents, the saint left the sinner before a crucifix. Upon returning, he found the man weeping for his sins.

If we need to feel greater sorrow of soul, let us gaze on the crucifix! Let us picture Christ's face—pale, covered with perspiration and blood, His eyes almost closed in death;

let us look upon those ribs laid bare, listen to the agonizing death rattle, think of the torments of His soul, and in spirit kiss His feet and hands. The crucifixion is the work of our sins.

The lukewarm soul is aroused by meditating on the crucifixion. The cross of Christ moves even the most indifferent hearts. Only the obstinate, the spiritually blind, and the deaf to grace are able to resist it.

Some who are not shaken by the thought of purgatory are moved by the passion of Christ.

One such person confided to his director: "I had abandoned myself to a life of tepidity and indifference interwoven with voluntary imperfections. However, I had kept the practice of making the stations of the cross, especially on the Fridays of Lent. One day, at the twelfth station I seemed to hear this silent plea from the crucifix: *See how much I have suffered for you! With your sacrifices help Me to save souls! Love Me as I have loved you!*

"I came to myself, wept bitterly over my state, and began to live a life of fervor."

If someone needs to regain fervor in his spiritual life, let him put his finger into the wounds of the Savior, and place his hand in His side. The devotee of the Crucified progresses much.

✿

The most fruitful means of spiritual progress is meditation on the passion. From such meditation we learn how to practice all the virtues to perfection. Grace descends into our soul in abundance. A special attraction overcomes us, as Jesus promised: "And I, if I be lifted up from the earth, will draw all things to myself" (Jn. 12:32).

When we meditate on the passion of the Lord, three thoughts should take hold of us: Who suffered? For whom did He suffer? How much did He suffer?

It was the Son of God Who suffered: the Innocent One, the Holy One — not a sinner.

He suffered for me — also for others, it is true, but still He suffered everything for me: "who loved me and gave himself up for me" (Gal. 2:20).

And how greatly He suffered! Some souls find it hard to understand the sorrow and agony of the spirit of Christ Jesus. He shed all His blood for all of us alike — notwithstanding what He foresaw — that sinners would damn themselves: "What gain would there be from my lifeblood?" (Ps. 29:10) But Jesus saw as well many souls who would love Him greatly and would save themselves; He died for them, for all, for each and everyone of us, undergoing a special pain for each of our sins.

May such meditation bear fruit: sentiments of love and firm resolutions to live a holy life. Let us lament our sins, shake off our tepidity or revive our fervor.

The crucifix is the great book of the elect. St. Paul declared: "I determined not to know anything...except Jesus Christ and him crucified" (1 Cor. 2:2).

Inflamed with zeal for the salvation of souls, St. Francis Xavier reflected, "Down in the distant Orient, there are many souls who do not yet enjoy the benefits of the divine Blood." And he wanted It to bring the fruits of salvation to all.

# Christ —
## the God Man —
## Atoned for Our Sins  — 1

In the beginning was the Word, and the Word was with God; and the Word was God. He was in the beginning with God. All things were made through him, and without him was made nothing that has been made. In him was life, and the life was the light of men. And the light shines in the darkness; and the darkness grasped it not.

There was a man, one sent from God, whose name was John. This man came as a witness, to bear witness concerning the light, that all might believe through him. He was not himself the light, but was to bear witness to the light. It was the true light that enlightens every man who comes into the world. He was in the world, and the world knew him not. He came unto his own, and his own received him not. But to as many as received him he gave the power of becoming sons of God; to those who believe in his name: Who were born not of blood, nor of the will of the flesh, nor of the will of man, but of God.

And the Word was made flesh, and dwelt among us. And we saw his glory — glory as of the only-begotten of the Father — full of grace and of truth. John bore witness concerning him, and

19

cried, "This was he of whom I said, 'He who is to come after me has been set above me, because he was before me.'" And of his fullness we have all received, grace for grace. For the Law was given through Moses; grace and truth came through Jesus Christ. No one has at any time seen God. The only-begotten Son, who is in the bosom of the Father, he has revealed him.

Jn. 1:1-18

Let us consider the threefold preparation which was made for the passion: preparation by the Father, by Jesus Christ, and by men.

The Eternal Father prepared His Son for the great sacrifice: "God sent his son, born of a woman" (Gal. 4:4).

One day Abraham received a command from the Lord to offer up his only son Isaac in sacrifice. At first thought, this was incomprehensible, since the same God had repeatedly promised to make Abraham the father of a great nation, and now He was commanding the patriarch to sacrifice his only son!

Yet Abraham did not doubt. He spent a terrible night, fighting an inner battle: on the one hand, his fatherly heart tormented him; on the other, God had given him an explicit command. But the conclusion of all his thoughts was a firm trust in God; if he obeyed Him, the Lord would not fail to fulfill His promise. So Isaac set out for the mountain with his father.

*An angel stopped Abraham
as he was about to perform
the sacrifice--but the
Incarnate Son of God
was really offered.*

As he climbed, bearing the bundle of wood for the sacrifice, the boy looked at the knife for the immolation and asked: "Father, you have the fire and the wood, but where is the sheep for the holocaust?" (cf. Gen. 22:7) He knew nothing of God's command. His father had not had the heart to tell him about it, although he was on his way to execute it.

In the same manner, the Heavenly Father prepared His Son, as the great Victim. Let us note, however, that an angel stopped Abraham as he was about to perform the sacrifice. But the Incarnate Son of God was really offered; the sacrifice was accomplished in the Paschal Mystery.

Marvelous indeed is the picture of the Eternal Father presenting His crucified Son to the world: "For God so loved the world that he gave his only-begotten Son" (Jn. 3:16).

It was the Father Who willed the sacrifice, in expiation for the sin of Adam and for those of all humanity. In fact, it was necessary that either God would forgive, forgetting the sin; or that man would offer himself. Otherwise, all would be lost, since all had contracted original sin.

A way was undertaken in which justice and mercy were reconciled by the divine wisdom.

Divine justice would be satisfied; pardon would be granted to man; there would be a sacrifice of infinite value to satisfy the infinite malice of sin. But since man is finite, the God-Man would atone for the sins of all men.

The Son presented Himself to the Father and said: "Behold I come...to do your will, O God" (Heb. 10:7). Holocausts of goats and of lambs do not satisfy You, "but a body you have fitted to me" (Heb. 10:5). The Father gave the Son a body: "the power of the Most High shall overshadow you" (Lk. 1:35), so that He could suffer and die.

Thus the Father prepared the Victim, and willed Its total immolation, for the wrath of heaven against the sinner is great, as Scripture tells us.

From Adam to Christ, how many prophecies referred to Jesus! His whole life was prophesied: the time and place of His birth, the Magi, the hatred of Herod.... But above all the prophecies referred to His life of suffering; that is, to the last week of the life of Christ, from Palm Sunday to Good Friday. They foretold that He would be betrayed, scourged, insulted, condemned, and crucified between two robbers. All is foretold, in every circumstance. The Father prepared the Victim, the Host for the Sacrifice.

In Gethsemane, the Heavenly Father sent the chalice of the passion to His Son: He chose not to grant the prayer to remove the chalice from Him—the chalice of insults, lashes, thorns, condemnation and death on the cross after excruciating agony.

It appears to us that a father is unmoved by the groans of his son, as if he has suddenly become cruel towards his son, in order to show mercy solely to the sinner. Now, it is sufficient for a repentant sinner to shed one tear in order to obtain God's pardon. Then, instead, the Son did not move the Father to pity with all His bloody sweat.

There was a ritual among the Hebrews, in which the high priest, in the presence of all the people, would impose his hands on a large wild goat, which he afterwards drove out into the wilderness to be devoured by wild beasts. Symbolically, all the sins of the people were heaped upon this goat.

However, that ritual was symbolic only. But in the Garden of Gethsemane, the Heavenly Father, not the high priest, actually heaped the sins of all humanity upon His Son. "He was pierced for our offenses, crushed for our sins" (Is. 53:5). He was crushed by them like a worm. "And it was our infirmities that he bore" (Is. 53:4). He bore our iniquities and He paid our debts: "He himself bore our sins..." (1 Pt. 2: 24). He who had not known sin, was treated as the great sinner, struck down by God and humiliated.

The Eternal Father contemplated the scene of Calvary: Jesus stripped of His garments, knocked roughly to the ground, nailed to the cross, and raised up in the sight of all. But He did not come to free Him; neither did He send a ram as a substitute for the Son, as He had done for Abraham. "My God, my God, why have you forsaken me?" (Mk. 15:34) Let us try to penetrate this great mystery.

This preparation for the passion of Christ, was the result of our sins: "And it was our infirmities that he bore" (Is. 53:4). They are the cause of the death of the divine Son. Which of us is innocent? No one, except the Blessed Virgin; however, she received a more plentiful redemption, having been preserved from original sin in view of the death of Jesus Christ.

# Christ —
# the God Man —
# Atoned for Our Sins   — 2

The Son, as well as the Father, prepared for the Paschal Mystery. Jesus Christ was born to die. He came from heaven, took a body, and was born to redeem us. That was His mission.

The entire life of Christ was a cross and martyrdom — daily martyrdom in preparation for the final sacrifice. "For us men and for our salvation He came down from heaven; and was conceived by the Holy Spirit of the Virgin Mary and was made man.... He was crucified, died, and was buried!" (Nicene Creed)

Jesus prophesied His passion several times: "Behold, we are going up to Jerusalem, and the Son of Man will be betrayed...to the Gentiles to be mocked and scourged and crucified..." (cf. Mt. 20:18-19).

When He was transfigured on Tabor, and Moses and Elia came to speak with Him, they discussed what would soon take place in Jerusalem; that is, the passion.

Jesus saw and foretold every detail of His passion; but His disposition was always the same: "I have not come to do my will but your will" (cf. Jn. 6:38; Heb. 10:9).

Woe to anyone who tried to dissuade Him! When Peter did not wish to hear Him speak of suffering and of death, He aimed these terrible words at him: "Get behind me, satan, you are a scandal to me" (Mt. 16:23). And similarly, when Peter, still not understanding the heart of the Master, tried to defend Him with a sword in the Garden of Gethsemane, Jesus reproved him anew, saying: "Shall I not drink the cup that the Father has given me?" (Jn. 18:11).

During His ministry, Jesus was readying Himself for the great moment. "But I have a baptism to be baptized with; and how distressed I am until it is accomplished!" (Lk. 12:50) He suffered because His hour was still distant. He had an immense desire to suffer, in order to redeem humanity and to carry out His heroic obedience to the Father.

Whenever Jesus thought ahead to His passion, He seemed to lose His ordinary way of acting, as if He knew not how to contain Himself. When going to Jerusalem for the sacrifice, He did not walk among the Apostles. Usually He stayed in their midst, instructing them as they moved along. Now He preceded them, walking on alone so quickly that no one could keep up with Him: "and Jesus was walking in front of them" (Mk. 10:32), so quickly that the Apostles were amazed, never having seen Him in such a hurry: "and they were in dismay" (Mk. 10:32).

After the Last Supper had been celebrated and Judas had left the Cenacle, Jesus went to the Garden of Gethsemane. Although He knew that Judas and the mob would come right to that spot, He did not go elsewhere.

Jesus' proximate preparation for His passion began in the Garden, when He magnanimously said to His followers: "Rise, let us go" (Mt. 26:46). And He went forth to meet His betrayer and His passion: "Behold, he who betrays me is at hand" (Mt. 26:46).

And we, on the other hand, sometimes flee in fear in the face of a little suffering! How different is our heart from that of Jesus! St. Peter wrote: "Christ also has suffered for you, leaving you an example that you may follow in his steps" (1 Pt. 2:21). St. Augustine says: "He who would form the martyrs, wished to become the first and greatest martyr."

The Apostles had willingly eaten the Last Supper with the Lord, but when it came to suffering with Him, they all fled.

Some souls, while loving the devotion to the Crucified, do not love suffering. Woe to anyone who lays a cross on their shoulders!

In the Acts of the Apostles, on the other hand, we read of the courage of the Apostle Paul: "And now, behold, I am going to Jerusalem, compelled by the Spirit, not knowing what will happen to me there; except that in every city the Holy Spirit warns me, saying that imprisonment and persecution are awaiting me. But I fear none of these, nor do I count my life more precious than myself, if only I may accomplish my course and the ministry that I have received from the Lord Jesus, to bear witness to the gospel of the grace of God" (Acts 20:22-24).

And what of ourselves? Do we have the courage to make penance? Such is our duty. The *Apostolic Constitution on Indulgences* promulgated by Pope Paul VI declares:

"It is necessary for the full remission and — as it is called — reparation of sins not only that friendship with God be reestablished by a sincere conversion of the mind and amends made for the offense against His wisdom and goodness, but also that all the personal as well as social values and those of the universal order itself, which have been diminished or destroyed by sin, be fully integrated *whether through voluntary reparation which will involve punishment or through acceptance of the punishments established by the just and most holy wisdom of God,* from which there will shine forth throughout the world the sanctity and the splendor of His glory.... For all men who walk this earth daily commit at least venial sins; thus all need the mercy of God to be set free from the penal consequences of sin."

It is a penance to accept and to fulfill well one's own duty in life.

Men, too, prepared the passion of Jesus Christ—first of all, His enemies.

It is heartbreaking to think that the Son of God had come to save humanity, and men rejected Him: "Away with him! Away with him! Crucify him!" (Jn. 19:15). In a rage, they shouted: "We do not wish this man to be king over us" (Lk. 19:14).

We, too, lose our heads when we sin.

Jesus had worked miracles; His goodness had won everyone. The crowds following Him had so hungered for His words as to forget food itself. Jealous and full of rancor, His enemies then sought to trap Him in His speech, so that they might accuse Him.

After the resurrection of Lazarus, the Sanhedrin met: "Do you see that we avail nothing? Behold, the entire world has gone after him!"

(Jn. 12:19) And the high priest, prophesying, declared: "It is expedient for us that one man die for the people, instead of the whole nation perishing" (Jn. 11:50). These words were true, but in a higher sense: one had to die, and Jesus would do so, that man might be saved.

They condemned Him. And Judas made his appearance, offering to deliver Him into their hands. The sacrilegious contract was sealed: on the one side was a little money, while the merchandise, bargained for at such a low price, was the Son of God. From then on Judas sought an opportune moment to hand Him over. He knew where they would all be on that Thursday night, and said: "Whomever I kiss, that is he; lay hold of him, and lead him safely away" (Mk. 14:44). The sentence pronounced tumultuously during that night tribunal was: "He is liable to death!" (Mt. 26:66)

Let us excite ourselves to a deep gratitude for the Redemption, and recite the sorrowful mysteries of the Rosary with devotion.

# The Unfolding
# of the
# Paschal Mystery

And when the hour had come, he reclined at table, and the twelve apostles with him. And he said to them, "I have greatly desired to eat this passover with you before I suffer; for I say to you that I will eat of it no more, until it has been fulfilled in the kingdom of God." And having taken a cup, he gave thanks and said, "Take this and share it among you; for I say to you that I will not drink of the fruit of the vine, until the kingdom of God comes."

And having taken bread, he gave thanks and broke, and gave it to them, saying, "This is my body, which is being given for you; do this in remembrance of me." In like manner he took also the cup after the supper, saying, "This cup is the new covenant in my blood, which shall be shed for you." Lk. 22:14-20

"At the Last Supper," states the *Constitution on the Sacred Liturgy,* "on the night when He was betrayed, our Savior instituted the Eucharistic Sacrifice of His Body and Blood. He did this in order to perpetuate the sacrifice of the cross throughout the centuries

33

until He should come again, and so to entrust to His beloved spouse, the Church, a memorial of His death and resurrection: a sacrament of love, a sign of unity, a bond of charity, a paschal banquet in which Christ is eaten, the mind is filled with grace, and a pledge of future glory is given to us."

The Holy Mass is prefigured at least three times in the Old Testament: in the sacrifice of Melchisedec, with the offering of bread and wine; in the manna which sustained the Hebrews for many years during their journey through the desert, "the bread from heaven endowed with all delights" (Wis. 16:20), a symbol of Holy Communion; and in the tabernacle in the Temple of Jerusalem, where the cloud which sometimes covered the tabernacle and filled the Temple prefigured the Real Presence of Jesus Christ in the Holy Eucharist.

The preparation for the first Mass was a work of the ages, culminating in the actions of Jesus Christ.

When Jesus preached the Good News to the crowds in the Palestinian countryside, He foretold the great mystery of the Eucharist, especially in the miraculous multiplication of the loaves, and in the discourse recorded in the sixth chapter of St. John's Gospel: "I am the living bread that has come down from heaven.

*Christ entrusted to the Church*
*a memorial of His death and resurrection:*
*a sacrament of love, a sign of unity,*
*a bond of charity, a paschal banquet*
*in which Christ is eaten,*
*the mind is filled with grace,*
*and a pledge of future glory is given to us.*

If anyone eat of this bread he shall live forever.... He who eats my flesh and drinks my blood has life everlasting" (Jn. 6:51, 55).

Jesus was preparing for the Last Supper, and He wanted His Apostles to be prepared also. He ardently looked forward to the great sacrifice. It was because of His desire to be baptized in the baptism of His blood, that He quickened His pace on that last journey toward Jerusalem. He would give man the last sign: the supreme sign of His love; therefore He had the Apostles prepare the great upper room, adorning it for the Last Supper.

Let us think of the sentiments of the heart of Jesus at the Last Supper. About to leave the Apostles, He was torn between two desires; He longed to remain with them and at the same time He ardently desired to return to the Father—as the Father Himself willed.

Thus out of His love for the Father and for us, Christ was about to institute a divinely ingenious way to stay with men and yet depart from them. Thus He would always remain among us: "I am with you all days, even unto the consummation of the world" (Mt. 28:20).

The sacraments of Holy Eucharist and Holy Orders which Jesus was about to institute, would foster man's love for God and neighbor: an ardent love of God in which the whole heart is reserved for Him, and a love of neighbor symbolized in the washing of the feet.

A great mystery of goodness and humility was accomplished at the Last Supper by Jesus, Who knelt before His Apostles to wash their feet. The astonished Peter did not want the Master to perform this humiliating action, but Jesus in His wisdom overcame his objections. Then He concluded: "You call me Master and Lord, and you say well, for so I am. If therefore I, the Lord and Master, have washed your feet, you also ought to wash the feet of one another" (Jn. 13:13-14).

This is an occasion for exercising faith. As human beings we have our rights, but as Christians, let us yield to our brothers by making acts of humility, imitating our Master. Let us gain the merit of charity.

If we allow ourselves to be led by human wisdom, this could seem exaggeration. But if we acquire the wisdom of the Lord Jesus, our reasoning will transcend the merely human and conform itself to His. And then we will accept even blame with an unclouded countenance and a smile.

Let us pause to consider the contrast between, on the one hand, the great love of the tremendous heart of Jesus for men; and, on the other, the fierce hatred of men against Him.

St. Paul says: "On the night in which he was betrayed..." (1 Cor. 11:23). Jesus had chosen precisely that night for the institution of the Holy Eucharist. Driven from the world, He had decided to remain in the world always: "Behold, I am with you all days" (Mt. 28:20).

The Savior knew that Judas had already made his treasonous contract with the priests of the Sanhedrin. They had agreed to pay thirty pieces of silver, and were waiting for Him to be delivered into their hands before giving Judas the sum. However, Jesus was not to be put to death on the feast, lest the people who loved Him begin to riot or defend Him.

Human foolishness! The Savior of mankind had come from heaven to bring every good upon the earth, and what a reception He was given! Should it surprise us, then, if the follower of Christ is persecuted, if his work is opposed, if his efforts to do good are often canceled out, while evil is accepted and even acclaimed?

Jesus foresaw clearly what would happen that night: "Strike the shepherd that the sheep may be dispersed" (Zach. 13:7). Indeed all the Apostles would flee, abandoning the Master: "Then all the disciples left him and fled" (Mt. 26:56).

What caused the Lord the greatest pain was His knowledge of how Peter would conduct himself that night. Peter, who had been His confidant—Peter who was to be the visible head of His Church—would deny Jesus Christ and would confirm his denial with an oath.

Oh, human weakness! The human heart is a mystery. It is necessary to have compassion on others, to pray for them and to help them—especially those who are most in need. Jesus loved all, but in a particular way He loved sinners, with whom He showed Himself most merciful.

His heart oppressed by this sorrowful vision of ingratitude and of abandonment, Jesus took bread between His hands, blessed it, broke it and offered it to the Apostles, saying: "Take and eat; this is my body" (Mt. 26:26). And, taking the chalice, raising His eyes to heaven, He blessed it and offered it, too, to the Apostles, saying to them: "All of you drink of this; for this is my blood of the new covenant, which is being shed for many unto the forgiveness of sins. Do this in remembrance of me" (Mt. 26:27-28; Lk. 22:19).

With these words Jesus instituted the Holy Eucharist and the priesthood. Both are the fruits of His love. Priests continue the work of Christ; in one part of the world after another the Eucharistic Jesus is offered for the salvation, comfort and relief of souls. Through priests men continue to receive the bread of the spirit, "lest they faint on the way" (Mt. 15:32). Thus Jesus Christ still repeats to all: "Come to me, all you who labor and are burdened, and I will give you rest" (Mt. 11:28).

In that moment, the divine Master looked into the centuries ahead and saw the men of all places and of all ages; for all and for each of them He offered Himself.

"The Most Blessed Eucharist," states the *Decree on the Ministry and Life of Priests*, "contains the entire spiritual boon of the Church, that is, Christ Himself, our Pasch and Living Bread, by the action of the Holy Spirit through His very flesh vital and vitalizing, giving life to men who are thus invited and encouraged to offer themselves, their labors and all created things, together with Him."

Let us ask the Lord to increase and strengthen our eucharistic devotion. Let us ask of Him the grace always to understand better and correspond more fully to this great gift, that one day we may be able to see Jesus Christ face to face.

Now what did Jesus see before Him? The Apostles were all fervently protesting their fidelity: "Lord, with you, I am ready to go both to prison and death" (Lk. 22:33). Yet the Master replied that they would abandon Him, and to Peter in particular He declared: "You will deny me" (Mt. 26:34).

At that moment acts of love welled up spontaneously in the Apostles' hearts and in their words. They believed that they were speaking sincerely, but Jesus saw that before long they would abandon Him, and Peter would deny Him.

And Judas also was present at the table of the Last Supper. The Eleven received Holy Communion; we do not know if Judas did. At any rate, Judas withdrew silently, in such a way that his absence was hardly noticed. He went to invite Jesus' enemies to come to Gethsemane to take Him, bind Him and conduct Him—first to prison and then to death. What sorrow! "One of you will betray me" (Jn. 13:21). Sometimes those for whom we have done the most, repay us with ingratitude. And then the heart suffers.

Seeing the ingratitude that the Apostles would show Him, did Jesus delay or suspend the institution of the sacrifice of love? Or, seeing that they would abandon Him, did He perhaps postpone their priestly ordination? Not at all; He accomplished all according to the will of the Father, regardless of the ingratitude of men.

It is here that we often err: we desire gratitude, since we do not work enough for God. We still have too many human views. Let us let the will of God — the will of the Heavenly Father — rule in us.

# "Rise
and
Pray" — 1

After saying these things, Jesus went forth
with his disciples beyond the torrent of Cedron,
where there was a garden called Gethsemane
into which he and his disciples entered. Now
Judas, who betrayed him, also knew the place,
since Jesus had often met there together with his
disciples.

But when he was at the place, he said to
them, "Sit down here, while I pray. Pray, that
you may not enter into temptation." And he took
with him Peter and James and John, and he began to feel dread and to be exceedingly troubled. Then he said to them, "My soul is sad,
even unto death. Wait here and watch with me."
And he himself withdrew from them about a
stone's throw, and fell on the ground, and began
to pray that, if it were possible, the hour might
pass from him; and he said, "Abba, Father, all
things are possible to you. Remove this cup from
me; yet not what I will, but what you will." And
there appeared to him an angel from heaven to
strengthen him. And falling into an agony he
prayed the more earnestly.

And his sweat became as drops of blood
running down upon the ground. And rising

from prayer he came to the disciples, and found them sleeping for sorrow. And he said to Peter, "Simon, do you sleep? Could you not, then, watch one hour with me?" And (to the others) "Why do you sleep? Rise and pray, that you may not enter into temptation. The spirit indeed is willing, but the flesh is weak." Again a second time he went away and prayed, saying the same words over: "My Father, if this cup cannot pass away unless I drink it, your will be done." And they did not know what answer to make to him. And leaving them he went back again, and prayed a third time, saying the same words over.

Mt. 26:36-44; Mk. 14:32-41; Lk. 22:39-46; Jn. 18:1-2

After the Last Supper, Jesus set out toward Gethsemane. But first, with the Apostles, he recited a hymn of thanksgiving and his priestly prayer, in which he prayed for himself, the Apostles and the Church.

Prayers for oneself are those most easily fulfilled. Let us pray for ourselves in the first place; we have so many needs! Some souls are very sure of themselves; they think that they are already good!

Let us pray for ourselves; let us feel the need of God; let us allow Him to help us day by day, moment by moment. In peace and serenity let us examine our lack of correspondence, knowing that we have still responded too poorly to the grace of God; let us ask pardon for our infidelities and transgressions. If we

had been better, if we had corresponded mor
to grace, how much more good could we hav
done! How much more efficacious would ou
apostolate be if each one of us were "he whos
hands are sinless, whose heart is clean" (Ps
23:4).

Jesus then prayed for the Apostles. Let u
pray for priests, since the fervor and salvatio
of the faithful depend greatly upon them. The
are the captains of the Christian army. Th
fostering of priestly vocations is a greatly meri
torious undertaking.

Thirdly, Jesus prayed for the Church. Le
us, too, pray for the Church, that she may grow
For hundreds of years some nations have ex
ploited millions of men, holding them unde
the yoke of tyranny, but this is greed. Th
Church, instead, makes her conquests in orde
to do good, to diffuse the doctrine and the king
dom of Christ in the minds and hearts of al
men. The *Decree on the Mission Activity o
the Church* declares: "In the present state o
affairs, out of which there is arising a new situ
ation for mankind, the Church, being the sal
of the earth and the light of the world (cf. Mt
5:13-14), is more urgently called upon to save
and renew every creature, that all things may
be restored in Christ and all men may consti
tute one family in him and one people of God.'

*Let us, too, pray
for the Church,
that she may grow.*

Arriving in the Garden of Olives, the Master divided His Apostles into two groups; eight He left at the entrance; three He led further on. These three were more dear to Him; they were souls whom He loved greatly, not from natural inclinations, but because they had always been generous with Him. Peter represented faith; James, deeds; and John, love. Already these chosen ones had witnessed their Master's transfiguration on Mt. Tabor. "Wait here," He told them now, "and watch with me" (Mt. 26:38).

Jesus loved the solitude of the deserts and mountains where He habitually immersed Himself in intimacy with God.

He prayed; He had many things to say to the Father that night! At this, His entrance into the passion, His soul was downcast, grief-stricken, anguished. "He began to feel dread and to be exceedingly troubled" (Mk. 14:33).

Alone, prostrate on the ground, He felt Himself oppressed by the thought of His passion. He was pained and saddened by all the sins that weighed Him down—sins which the Father had heaped upon Him, almost identifying Him with them.

We, too, weighed heavily upon the heart of the Lord that night; we, too, contributed to His agony—we whom He has chosen to be close to Him!

*If I had been betrayed by an enemy, I could bear it; but you, to whom I have given all of Myself, whom I have made sharer of all My gifts...this is the greatest pain!*

Jesus' agony was intensified by the thought of the countless souls who would be snatched from Him by the fallen angels and dragged into hell. The burden weighing upon Him grew heavier: "The cords of the nether world enmeshed me" (Ps. 17:6).

# "Rise and Pray" — 2

If a divine strength had not sustained the Savior, He would have died in Gethsemane, from that consideration of how many souls would be damned notwithstanding His passion: "What gain would there be from my life-blood?" (Ps. 29:10)

He prayed, "Father, if it is possible, let this cup pass away from me; yet not my will but yours be done" (Lk. 22:42). And in this He taught us a lesson in prayer.

We should ask for the graces that seem profitable for us — material and especially spiritual — but let us add, as Jesus did: "Not my will but yours be done" (Lk. 22:42), because it may very well be that the Lord wants to give us other graces, much more useful to us. We do not know what is best for ourselves, but God knows. If the Heavenly Father wishes instead to give us graces different from those which we want, let us allow Him to do it, and abandon ourselves to His fatherly care: "Cast all your anxiety upon him, because he cares for you" (1 Pt. 5:7). What we must seek above all is our sanctification.

Let us dispose ourselves to do the will of God, once it is manifest and certain. At times it is more difficult to do the will of God under simple, ordinary circumstances than it is in great matters which demand more sacrifice. However, we should exercise patience in these small matters especially. Great occasions are great because they are exceptional; instead small occasions are continuous.

Every day there is that particular will of God to be carried out; there are those annoyances to be borne with. There are contradictions, and internal or external disturbances which are not great in themselves, but are made so by their continuity. Heroism consists precisely in bearing with these.

Oftentimes more love is shown for God by gazing heavenward or looking upon a crucifix to draw strength in a situation of minor importance, than is shown when the sacrifice asked is so great that it is glorious to accomplish, and one fortifies oneself with prayer in expectation. When someone is always disposed to accept small sacrifices, small mortifications, and small ill humors, then that soul is abandoned in God. Thus, it can truly say: "Your will be done on earth as it is in heaven" (Mt. 6:10).

Faith is not complete if it lacks the disposition of doing the will of God, whatever it may be. But when faith is true and there is love of God in the heart, the Lord listens to the one who prays; and gives that soul whatever is most useful for growth in holiness.

We may be sure that Jesus Christ loves us more than we love ourselves; let us have confidence in Him.

Feeling the need of comfort, the Savior arose from His prayer and went to seek consolation from the Apostles. But He found them asleep, indifferent to the profound sadness of their Master.

He reproved them: "Could you not, then, watch one hour with me?... Pray that you may not enter into temptation" (Mt. 26:40-41). And He returned to pray to the Father.

So great was the anxiety of His heart, that His blood pulsed to its extremity, and flowed out from the pores of His skin. It trickled down over His body and soaked into the ground beneath Him.

Rising up, Jesus returned to His Apostles, but once again He found them sleeping. At the sound of another reproof, they tried to rouse themselves, but soon after He left them, they fell asleep again. Jesus was at the point of death. Generally, not even one who is dying sweats blood. And the Apostles slept!

It was heartrending—that abandonment which Jesus suffered from men—and yet they were His friends and confidants: "I have called you friends" (Jn. 15:16). Shortly before, He had fed them with His Body and most precious Blood, at which time He had foretold their ingratitude. They had made many protests of their love; now, instead, they had abandoned Him to Himself.

Coming back from praying a third time, the Master urged them: "Rise, let us go. Behold, he who betrays me is at hand!" (Mt. 26:46)

Spiritual desolation is an obscuring of the spirit, a disturbance, a strong enticement toward low or earthly things. It can come in the form of disquietude, agitation of heart, fear of not being saved, doubt of having been heard in prayer, a sense of desperation with regard to God, or privation of every interior comfort. Then one feels a sort of grief, tepidity, torpor and boredom in the service of God and in spiritual things.

Sometimes the soul itself is at fault: because it is tepid, lazy and negligent in its prayer life; because venial faults like vanity and self-

*If one feels himself alone,*
*he should revive his faith,*
*reflecting that God is nearer then,*
*than He is at other times....*

love, are given in to easily; because there is a lack of generosity in corresponding to grace. At other times this difficulty comes as a trial from God, as was the desolation suffered by St. Alphonsus Liguori when he was about ninety, or that of St. Teresa of Avila, which lasted fifteen years. At some point in life, every saint has undergone this spiritual desolation for a period of time.

It is the rule of the saints that no resolution is to be abandoned during these trying moments, and no practice is to be omitted; one should carry out all his previous resolutions with constancy. It is precisely at such a time that prayer, meditation, examination of conscience and mortification of the senses must be intensified.

If one feels himself alone, he should revive his faith, reflecting that God is nearer then, than He is at other times, and His grace is always proportional to the need. Will power and one's own strength are better tested when one has to fight against the current. A serene blue sky will follow upon the darkness; the Lord will again make Himself felt, accompanied by an increase of grace and spiritual comfort.

St. James the Apostle asks: "Is any one of you sad?" (Jas. 5:13) He does not recommend that such a one divert himself, joke, walk, converse, play music, and so forth. Rather, he says: "Let him pray" (Jas. 5:13). And the Gospel says of Jesus: "And falling into an agony, he prayed the more earnestly" (Lk. 22:43). He prayed the longer. Then He was comforted by an angel: "An angel strengthened him" (Lk. 22:43).

Here is the true consolation; let one especially turn to the crucifix: "Passion of Christ, comfort me; O good Jesus, hear me; within Your wounds hide me; permit me not to be separated from You."

Some souls are always inconstant. If the Lord tries them for a moment, they abandon all, becoming confused, agitated and despairing.

Instead, stability of spirit at every moment is a sign of real virtue. Everything in life is changeable; but the soul who truly loves God is unaffected by such changes and remains serene, since he gazes on high, beyond the clouds and tempest, always contemplating the fatherly face of God—Whom he wishes only and always to please. God will never fail him.

If at some time the Lord Jesus gives us a share in His anguish, abandonment and afflictions, He is giving us a token of His predilection. Let us bear with everything and have trust — all else notwithstanding — hoping against hope. Sacred Scripture says: "A patient man need stand firm but for a time, and then contentment comes back to him" (Sir. 1:20).

# Peace and Happiness from the Cross

They therefore led Jesus from Caiphas to the praetorium. Now it was early morning, and they themselves did not enter the praetorium, that they might not be defiled, but might eat the passover.

Pilate therefore went outside to them, and said, "What accusation do you bring against this man?" They said to him in answer, "If he were not a criminal we should not have handed him over to you." Pilate therefore said to them, "Take him yourselves, and judge him according to your law." The Jews, then, said to him, "It is not lawful for us to put anyone to death." This was in fulfillment of what Jesus had said, indicating the manner of his death.

And they began to accuse him, saying, "We have found this man perverting our nation, and forbidding the payment of taxes to Caesar, and saying that he is Christ a king."

Pilate therefore again entered into the praetorium, and said to him, "Are you the king of the Jews?" Jesus answered, "Do you say this of yourself, or have others told you of me?" Pilate answered, "Am I a Jew? Your own people and the chief priests have delivered you to me. What have you done?" Jesus answered, "My kingdom is not of this world. If my kingdom were of this world, my followers would have fought that I might not be delivered to the Jews. But, as it is, my kingdom is not from here." Pilate therefore said to him, "Then you are a king?" Jesus answered, "You have said it; I am a king. This is why I was born, and why I have come into the world, to bear witness to the truth. Everyone who is of the truth hears my voice."

Mt. 27:11; Mk. 5:2; Lk. 23:2-3; Jn. 18:28-38

Now Jesus stood before the tribunal, which had gathered in haste during the night. Accusations were being hurled from all sides, one contradicting another, for "their evidence did not agree" (Mk. 14:59).

The high priest, determined to condemn Jesus, claimed to do so in the name of the Mosaic law: "I adjure you by the living God that you tell us whether you are the Christ, the Son of God" (Mt. 26:63).

Jesus knew that His condemnation and death hung upon His reply. And He gave it: "You have said it. Nevertheless, I say to you, hereafter you shall see the Son of Man sitting at the right hand of the Power and coming upon the clouds of heaven" (Mt. 26:64).

Even though this declaration would certainly be taken as a pretext for condemnation by the Sanhedrin, Jesus had not remained silent. Sometimes we must say something which will cost sacrifice; we must do something which will be wrongly interpreted. One who directs others must surely know that he will be criticized and judged wrongly, no matter who he is. The holiest of men and those who have imitated Jesus the most also fall prey to evil misunderstandings and condemnations. Many have even hoped for their death!

This was especially so with Jesus, therefore, He being most holy. They wanted His death at any cost.

They had already tried to trap Him in His speech: *If He says that we must pay the tribute to Caesar, we will say that He is a friend of Rome and have Him condemned by the Pharisees, and if He says that we do not have to pay the tribute to Caesar, we will accuse Him before the Emperor as a revolutionary, who does not want the government of Rome. No matter how He replies He will die.*

Then, Jesus had freed Himself from their trap with ease, but now He knew that His time had come. Before, He had said: "My hour has not yet come" (Jn. 2:4): *It is useless for you to tempt me.* Even when they had gone to lay hands on Him and hurl Him over the precipice, He had vanished from their midst, and when they had sought to stone Him, the rocks had fallen from their hands.

But now He knew that the hour had come: "This is your hour and the power of darkness" (Lk. 22:53). It was the hour of His enemies. It was the hour willed by the Father and, therefore, He bore witness to the truth.

How many times the follower of Christ is in a position where loyalty to the Lord costs him much in the eyes of men. At times, therefore, an interior struggle takes place in one's heart. Woe to him who does not reflect: *I want to do the will of God—my duty—whether I like it or not, whether others like it or not.*

Jesus Christ Himself did not please everyone when He called His adversaries a: "brood of vipers!" (Mt. 3:7) He knew that they would be enraged—that His words would wound them deeply. "Hypocrites, why do you tempt me?" (Mt. 22:18) But this was His duty—the will of the Heavenly Father. It was His mission.

Now He acknowledged God before the high priest and Sanhedrin. And they rent their garments, as if they had heard a blasphemy against God: "You have heard the blasphemy? What do you think?" (Mk. 14:64) And all cried out together: "He is liable to death" (Mt. 26:66).

Is He Who is the Truth worthy of death? He Who will judge all? He Who gives life to all men?

And then that soldier, eager to please the high priest, raised his iron-clad fist and struck Jesus a blow on His face which made the cheeks become livid and blood issue from His mouth. And Jesus said nothing.

Do we know how to do the will of God? Do we not sometimes lose our peace of mind just because we have heard a word that stings or hurts us?

Those who were on guard that night taunted Jesus. They blindfolded Him, and took pleasure in striking Him with their fists and in covering His vesture and tunic with spittle. Then they challenged Him: "Prophesy to us, O Christ! Who is it that struck you?" (Mt. 26:68)

Did any complaint issue from Jesus' lips? Did He condemn those who treated Him thus? No—He, the innocent lamb, let Himself be led on to torture and did not shed a tear or voice a complaint.

The whole assembly arose, and binding Jesus, led Him to the governor, Pontius Pilate. They were more guilty than Pilate; because of the prophecies, the holiness of Christ's doctrine and His miracles, they should have recognized in Him the true Messias.

When someone has one talent more than others have, and does not make it bear fruit for the Lord, what a misfortune it is! When one has more education and is more mature in experience, and does not use this education and experience for God, what a misfortune it is! It would be better to be ignorant—better not to have that talent! It would be better not to have received certain graces than to waste them.

Jesus was handed over to Pilate, and all cried out against Him: "We have found this man perverting our nation, and forbidding the payment of taxes to Caesar, and saying that he is Christ a king." Pilate said to them, "Take him yourselves, and judge him according to your law." But they answered, "It is not lawful for us to put anyone to death." Pilate therefore again entered into the praetorium, summoned Jesus, and said to Him, "Are you the king of the Jews?" Jesus answered, "You have said it; I am a king. This is why I was born, and why I have come into the world.... My kingdom is not of this world. If my kingdom were of this world, my followers would have fought that I might not be delivered to the Jews. But, my kingdom is not from here" (cf. Lk. 23:2; Jn. 18:31-37).

Jesus Christ is King. He has three offices: Priest, Teacher and King. He is the Priest who immolated Himself. He accomplished this on the cross and He renews His sacrifice every day on our altars.

Jesus Christ is Teacher. He Himself proclaimed this several times and taught that He is the only Master. The devotion to Jesus, Master, is the most consoling of devotions.

Jesus Christ is King, and exercises His power over men's hearts. As King He can make, and has made, laws; He can and does exercise judicial power.

To His state as King corresponds our duty of obedience. We must serve Jesus, obey Him and please Him in the person of those who guide us.

The desire to please men is oftentimes the result of coldness towards Christ and lack of right intention. May grace, not nature, prevail in us! May a supernatural spirit, not personal preferences, reign in us! May we not be easier on ourselves than on others! Let us exercise more goodness towards those who are more needy and weak! Let us not cause others to lose merit, by making them love us too much. Let us love and serve the Lord; the Lord must be loved without measure.

To know how to suffer is really an art — the most important art in life. It is necessary to learn it and practice it; in practice, it will be perfected, like music or drawing.

One must advance from the easy to the difficult, from the small to the great. This is why

*The divine Master did not hide
the renunciation  which is in the cross,
but He revealed the peace and
happiness which comes from the cross.*

small pains are useful: they prepare us for greater sufferings, the last of which will result in our death. That will be like our own crucifixion and death.

It is true, but very seldom, that there may be an exception in which one is able to bear a grave difficulty, even though little crosses irritate and exasperate him. But, as a rule, one who does not joyfully accept small crosses, is easily disturbed by larger ones.

The mission of the elect soul is this: to witness to Christianity as a font of joy, not a font of melancholy.

The divine Master did not hide the renunciation which is in the cross, but He revealed the peace and happiness which comes from the cross. "Peace be to you... My peace I give you" (Lk. 24:36; Jn. 14:27). And in the general program He set forth in the Sermon on the Mount, with divine psychology, He opened the way to men's hearts by pronouncing the *eight beatitudes: Blessed are the poor, the meek, the suffering....*

# He, the Just,
# Suffered for Us,
# the Unjust  —  1

Now when Herod saw Jesus, he was exceedingly glad; for he had been a long time desirous to see him, because he had heard so much about him, and he was hoping to see some miracle done by him. Now he put many questions to him, but he made him no answer.

Now the chief priests and scribes were standing by, vehemently accusing him. But Herod, with his soldiery, treated him with contempt and mocked him, arraying him in a bright robe, and sent him back to Pilate. And Herod and Pilate became friends that very day; whereas previously they had been at enmity with each other.

Now at festival time the procurator used to release to the crowd a prisoner, whomever they would. Now he had at that time a notorious prisoner called Barabbas. Therefore, when they gathered together, Pilate said, "Whom do you wish that I release to you? Barabbas, or Jesus who is called Christ?" For he knew that they had delivered him up out of envy. Now, as he was sitting on the judgment-seat, his wife sent to him, saying, "Have nothing to do with that just man, for I have suffered many things in a dream

today because of him." But the chief priests and
the elders persuaded the crowds to ask for Barabbas and to destroy Jesus. But the procurator
addressed them, and said to them, "Which of the
two do you wish that I release to you?" And they
said, "Barabbas." Pilate said to them, "What
then am I to do with Jesus who is called Christ?"
They all said, "Let him be crucified!" The procurator said to them, "Why, what evil has he
done?" But they kept crying out the more, saying, "Let him be crucified!"

Now Pilate, seeing that he was doing no
good, but rather that a riot was breaking out,
took water and washed his hands in sight of the
crowd, saying, "I am innocent of the blood of
this just man; see to it yourselves." And all the
people answered and said, "His blood be on us
and on our children."

Then he released to them Barabbas; but
Jesus he scourged and delivered to them to be
crucified. Then the soldiers of the procurator
took Jesus into the praetorium, and gathered together about him the whole cohort. And they
stripped him and put on him a scarlet cloak; and
plaiting a crown of thorns, they put it upon his
head, and a reed into his right hand; and bend-
ing the knee before him they mocked him, saying, "Hail, King of the Jews!" And they spat on
him, and took the reed and kept striking him on
the head.

Mt. 27:15-30; Mk. 15:6-9; Lk. 23:4-25; Jn. 18:39-40; 19:1-3)

The pharisees had handed Jesus over out
of envy. Yes, they envied Jesus because He was
a younger doctor of the Law than they, and all
the people were following Him. "Behold the

entire world has gone after Him" (Jn. 12:19).
And instead of examining to see if He was
truly the Messias whom they should welcome,
they decided to put Him to death.

Envy is a vice which results in many
words, desires and actions which offend God.
The danger of this is ever present, deeply
rooted in our soul along with that of pride, and
easily makes itself felt. It may be enough for
two people to be together for one to conceive
feelings of envy against the other. Cain and
Abel exemplify this.

One who overcomes and conquers envy is
sure to progress greatly in a short time.

How often some individuals judge wrongly
and even make denunciations — out of envy!
"But why do you see the speck in your brother's
eye and yet do not consider the beam in your
own eye?" (Lk. 6:41)

To look upon others with hostility because
of their positions, successes, intelligence or
graces — all this is a consequence of envy. One
who is envious has no peace; a worm is gnaw-
ing at his heart.

We all admire those who always speak well
of others. Such individuals are happy that
others are esteemed or have better positions.
In the many occasions which arise in daily
life, these good souls generously console and

comfort those whom others, instead, might envy. David and Jonathan often came to each other's aid, whereas Saul was consumed by envy.

When there is something good in our neighbor, let us learn from it, rejoice in it and imitate it — not suffer from it!

Envy is a temptation. One who feels it should not consent, for the evil lies in giving in.

Jesus was led to Herod amidst the clamor and cries of the infuriated mob. How much He was suffering! Do we love Him? Do we feel the duty and need of making reparation? Who will share His agony and humiliation? Who will be so worthy? He who accustoms himself to daily suffering and knows the great science of the cross.

Herod was cunning and dishonest; Jesus had called him the "fox." This was the man who had ordered that John the Baptist be put to death at the instigation of that infamous woman Herodias — she who had the head of the saint brought to the table on a platter.

The ruler questioned Jesus at length, in an effort to satisfy his curiosity, and in the hope of seeing a miracle. But Jesus did not make any reply; He remained silent.

Sometimes silence is the best answer. One who keeps silence, says nothing; but in many cases he says much! Some people do not deserve an answer, nor should an answer be given. This is more for their sake than for ours; silence reproves them. In such a situation, it is better to say a *Hail Mary* than to answer.

Jesus was thought mad, and treated as such. Despising Him, Herod and his court made Him dress as a fool; then they sent Him back to Pilate. From that day on, Herod and Pilate, who had been enemies until then, were fast friends. Even enemies find themselves in accord when they are against Christ, for all of them are guided by the same leader: the Evil One.

That day Pilate was quite embarrassed, for the trial of Jesus was dragging on through the entire morning. What a difficult morning it was for Jesus, following a night of such torment!

Having found Jesus innocent, Pilate was seeking a way out of condemning Him. First he had sent Him to Herod, then he put up a delay with Barabbas:

"The chief priests and the elders persuaded the crowds to ask for Barabbas and to destroy Jesus. But the procurator addressed them, and said to them, 'Which of the two do you wish that I release to you?' And they said,

'Barabbas.' Pilate said to them, 'What then am I to do with Jesus who is called Christ?' They all said, 'Let him be crucified'" (Mt. 27:20-23). "So Pilate, wishing to satisfy the crowd, released to them Barabbas" (Mk. 15:15).

# He, the Just,
# Suffered for Us,
# the Unjust — 2

The crowd had had its way. When someone does not reason, when he is in a rage, when he is dominated by a passion, who can foresee the lengths to which he will go? Let us never deliberate when under the influence of anger; we will repent of it bitterly. At such times one does not take the counsel of prudence, but follows blind instinct.

Jesus was innocent; He was the incarnate Son of God. He had multiplied the bread and fed an immense multitude. He had given sight to the blind and hearing to the deaf. He had healed every sort of infirmity and had raised the dead. Jesus had gone about doing good to all! Barabbas, instead, was a revolutionary and a murderer; what evil had he not done! And yet to Barabbas was given the "Long live!" and to Jesus the cross. Irrational world!

Let us not rely on human justice, so false and unfair! Let us not expect recompense on this earth for good done! But this situation is for the best; thus we will not receive here below the reward which we want to receive eternal and full in heaven.

The saints prayed to remain in obscurity, in order to avoid every occasion of becoming vain.

God, the good and wise Father, gives us consolations to vivify us; and He gives us humiliations to ward off every danger of vanity. Vain complacency is very harmful! Those in high places may be tempted to this. To be in charge of others and to give orders means nothing other than being useful and practicing charity; more extensive duties are to be performed. Authority is to be exercised within a broader scope of charity.

Giving in to sin means preferring Barabbas to Jesus. It is crying out with the crowd: "Long live Barabbas; death to Jesus."

Pilate still would not call a halt to the proceedings; he questioned Jesus again. Then, not finding any fault in Him, he decided to have Him scourged in order to satisfy the people's thirst for blood.

He confessed Him innocent and sentenced Him to be scourged! Another contradiction! The innocent is not to be condemned! It is a crime to inflict punishment if there is no positive proof of guilt.

In the scourging, the soldiers competed with one another in striking harder. Through it all, the innocent Lamb did not utter a complaint — nothing! He remained silent:

"It was our infirmities that he bore, our sufferings that he endured, while we thought of him as stricken, as one smitten by God and afflicted. But he was pierced for our offenses, crushed for our sins; upon him was the chastisement that makes us whole, by his stripes we were healed. We had all gone astray like sheep, each following his own way, but the Lord laid upon him the guilt of us all. Though he was harshly treated, he submitted and opened not his mouth; like a lamb led to the slaughter or a sheep before the shearers, he was silent and opened not his mouth" (Isa. 53:4-7).

The Savior willed to expiate all our sins, and in the scourging, He especially atoned for those committed with the most widespread of the external senses, that of touch.

Let us picture to ourselves His body: the flesh shredded and the blood springing from every wound as the blows, which no one counted, continued to rain upon Him.

How highly has Jesus paid for our spirit of laziness and our readiness to give in to our senses! Let us try to make reparation for all the sins we have committed with our external senses. Let us offer the Lord some penances — at least those which daily life imposes upon us. We can, for instance, conquer the laziness of the morning. We can patiently put up with heat, fatigue and illness!

Jesus had remained silent. In this, too, He has a lesson for us. At times we may be falsely accused, as He was. Must we always defend and excuse ourselves? Must we blow up out of all proportion the harm which others do to us?

How can we still complain, when we have seen the Savior fall to the ground after the scourging, His strength sapped by loss of blood? How can we complain after seeing Him — loosed from the pillar — made to sit on a bench and subjected to a new torment?

The crowning with thorns was not one of the lawful punishments. Nonetheless, this· fiendish instrument of torture was placed on Jesus' head, and the soldiers struck it with·a reed, so that the thorns would penetrate more deeply. Then, to heap the offenses one on another, they came to pay Him homage with scornful genuflections, and to salute Him: "Hail, King of the Jews" (Mk. 15:18). *You wanted to make Yourself king; here is a crown: of thorns! You wanted to make Your-*

*self king; here is the purple: a rag draped over Your shoulders. You wanted to make Yourself king; here is a broken reed, symbol of command.*

What other man in this world was ever reduced to such a state?

In the crowning with thorns, Jesus especially expiated those sins which are committed with the faculties of mind and will. Let us reflect on the humiliation He bore to atone for thoughts of pride, and on the harsh treatment He endured to make reparation for thoughts of insubordination! Jesus expiated every thought contrary to faith and all the other virtues.

It was with indescribable pain that our Savior atoned for our sins of pride. We may have raised our heads above our equals; perhaps we have despised our inferiors; and we might have rebelled against our superiors.... But at how great a price!

Let us regret our foolishness. And if someone praises us, let us remain humble, thinking that if that person could see inside us and know all our faults — he would be likely to change his opinion soon enough.

However, it is not enough to avoid evil. We must add a positive endeavor, which consists in acquiring a true, tender and sincere love for

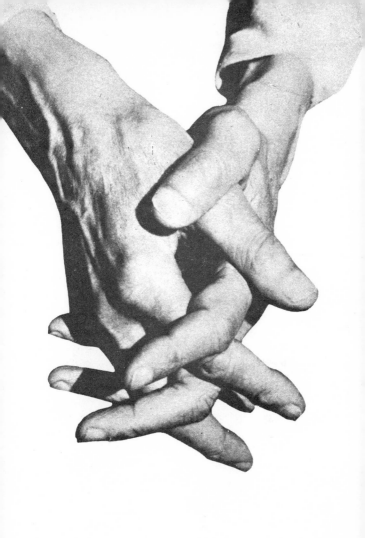

6. *Paschal Mystery*

*Let us love Jesus!
He has loved us
without limit;
let us not measure
our response.*

our Savior. Is there not something we can do for Him Who has spared nothing of Himself in doing so much for us? Let us resolve to love Him with *all* our mind, strength, heart and will.

Let us promise Him interior humility, submission and the spirit of obedience; let us promise Him that we will always conform our life to the divine wishes, thinking as God would have us think, and doing whatever the Lord points out to us through the commandments or the evangelical counsels or through the circumstances — pleasant or otherwise — in which we may find ourselves.

Let us love Jesus! He has loved us without limit; let us not measure our response. Let us love Him without reserve, wholeheartedly, above all else. Let us pardon the offenses of others, do good to those who hurt us, and pray for all.

Jesus accepted the scourging, crowning and derision for all of us. He foresaw our weaknesses, loss of time and thoughtlessness, and expiated all of them. Let us ask for a true horror of venial sin.

# By His Sufferings
# He Reconciled Us
# with the Father

Pilate therefore went outside and said to them, "Behold, I bring him out to you, that you may know that I find no guilt in him." Jesus therefore came forth, wearing the crown of thorns and the purple cloak. And he said to them, "Behold, the man!" When, therefore, the chief priests and the attendants saw him, they cried out, saying, "Crucify him! Crucify him!" Pilate said to them, "Take him yourselves and crucify him, for I find no guilt in him." The Jews answered him, "We have a Law, and according to that Law, he must die, because he has made himself Son of God."

Now when Pilate heard this statement, he feared the more. And he again went back into the praetorium, and said to Jesus, "Where are you from?" But Jesus gave him no answer. Pilate therefore said to him: "Do you not speak to me? Do you not know that I have power to crucify you, and that I have power to release you?" Jesus answered, "You would have no power at all over me were it not given you from above. Therefore, he who betrayed me to you has the greater sin."

And from then on Pilate was looking for a way to release him. But the Jews cried out, saying, "If you release this man, you are no friend of Caesar; for everyone who makes himself king sets himself against Caesar."

Pilate therefore, when he heard these words, brought Jesus outside, and sat down on the judgment-seat, at a place called Lithostrotos, but in Hebrew, Gabbatha. Now it was the Preparation Day for the Passover, about the sixth hour. And he said to the Jews, "Behold, your king!" But they cried out, "Away with him! Away with him! Crucify him!" Pilate said to them, "Shall I crucify your king?" The chief priests answered, "We have no king but Caesar." Now Pilate, seeing that he was doing no good, but rather that a riot was breaking out, took water and washed his hands in sight of the crowd, saying, "I am innocent of the blood of this just man; see to it yourselves." And all the people answered and said, "His blood be on us and on our children." Then he handed him over to them to be crucified. And so they took Jesus and led him away.

Mt. 19:24-25; Jn. 19:4-16

Great were the wrongs done to Jesus in preferring Barabbas to Him, in scourging Him and in crowning Him with thorns. Nevertheless, Pilate did not want to condemn Him to death; he understood the injustice of pronouncing the death sentence upon an innocent man, especially upon an innocence more resplendent than the light of the sun.

So Pilate sought another way out. He summoned Jesus and, seeing Him come forward in such a piteous state—lacerated, bruised and bleeding, with the purple rag upon His shoulders and the crown of thorns upon His head—the procurator was seized with compassion. Hoping that the rage of the people would cool when they, too, had seen Him, Pilate presented Jesus to them, saying: "Behold the man!" (Jn. 19:4)

But the people, on the contrary, were greatly enraged; they raised a more furious and menacing cry: "Crucify him! Crucify him!" (Jn. 19:5)

"Behold the man!"

The saints were deeply moved when considering this scene of the passion.

Some souls fear only punishments—temporal and eternal. Others, instead, are very sensitive, and are profoundly stirred when reflecting upon the sorrows of the Savior and the immense ingratitude that is sin. These souls are sensitive to the movements of grace. They live more out of love than of fear. And how about ourselves?

"Behold the man!" Behold that Jesus Who has loved you, has sanctified you in Baptism, has strengthened you in Confirmation, has given Himself to you as food in Holy Communion, and has pardoned you continually in the sacrament of Penance—that Jesus Who has offered all for you. Behold the Man of love!

And you, how do you respond when contemplating Jesus, so wounded for you? Let us respond: *Live and reign, Jesus, in the world and in our hearts.*

When one has taken the path of evil, he first walks it with a certain hesitation; he falls and picks himself up only to fall again; then he reaches a point in which his heart becomes hardened and his mind blinded, impenetrable to grace. Even in small matters, little vices and obstinacy, is blindness to be feared.

Pilate made a final interrogation of Jesus; He remained silent. The procurator, who must have been persuaded of His innocence by this time, became impatient and said: "Do you not speak to me? Do you not know that I have power to crucify you, and that I have power to release you?" (Jn. 19:10) Jesus replied: "You would have no power at all over me were it not given you from above. Therefore, he who betrayed me to you has the greater sin" (Jn. 19:11).

And Pilate, impressed by that firm declaration, sought some way to free Him. But while he was reflecting, the cries of the crowd from the square grew always more insistent: "Crucify him, crucify him!" (Jn. 19:6) "We have no king but Caesar" (Jn. 19:15). "If you release this man, you are no friend of Caesar" (Jn. 19:20). And Pilate condemned Jesus to death, for "saying he is Christ, a king" (Lk. 23:2).

Through cowardly fear of losing a position, and through human respect, Pilate had condemned the Innocent One to the death of the cross. Then he washed his hands, saying: "I am innocent of the blood of this just man" (Mt. 27:24). They were words incomprehensible and contradictory. Pilate was declaring himself innocent and yet he was condemning Jesus, Whom he proclaimed just.

When instigated by our passions, we combine the incompatible and contradictory.

He who sins prefers his own will, whims, passions and satisfaction to the will and holiness of Jesus, to heaven and to peace of soul. On one side are Jesus, paradise, grace and peace of soul; on the other, one's own satisfaction. What a shameful comparison! This is to place the most holy Jesus on a level with Barabbas, a revolutionary and a murderer—to compare holiness with greed and cruelty. Long live my passion; death to Jesus: in this does sin consist. At least Barabbas was a human being, but passion, instead, is something base and disgraceful. Nevertheless, one who sins cries out:

Long live my passion; who cares if I cast out Christ?

Yet the brow of Jesus was not darkened, nor was His expression troubled. He was thinking of how He would give His life to save us from hell.

Let us understand that sin is the cause of the death of Jesus Christ. Who now can feel innocent—who can deem himself prudent and worthy of regard, when he has condemned the Lord, crying: "Be crucified, Christ"?

Who deserves to be condemned to death? The sinner. Yet, this condemnation was given to Jesus Christ. Is it possible that we are still proud of ourselves—we, who are sinners? Is it possible that we still complain if sent to the second place, while we aspire to the first? Is it possible that we still expect to hold high positions and to be treated with regard? Would this be just? Would it be deserved?

Let us always be ready to say "It is a good thing, O Lord, that You have humiliated me." Yet pride, perhaps, will make us exclaim: "I don't deserve this!"

Sometimes one may be accused of a fault he has not committed.... But, on the other hand, how many *have* been committed that were not seen by others and not punished? If one has said only one lie in an entire lifetime, he should be sorry for it always. And, instead, there can be a life full of sins, imperfections and tepidity; should one, then, complain of not being understood?

In little sorrows, humiliations and mortifications let us thank the Lord, for thus we can suffer a little of purgatory here below; thus we can accompany the Redeemer in His sorrowful passion. It is better to make reparation here on earth, for besides their satisfactory value, little sufferings also have meritorious and impetratory value.

Let us be humble, and trustingly turn to the Heart of Jesus, that He may grant us His pardon, His love, His peace! Let us ask the Lord to grant us time to do penance and to obtain the plenary indulgence at the point of death.

In the prison there were two others who had been sentenced to the same punishment, but the heaviest of the three crosses was given to Jesus, as if He had committed the most serious crime. Yet this was He of whom it was said: "He has done all things well" (Mk. 7:37) — He Who "went about doing good and healing all" (Acts 10:37).

Of whom else was it ever said: *he has done all things well*? Jesus had gone about curing every physical and moral malady. And yet, He

*Weak Himself,*
*He was suffering*
*for the weak....*

had now been sentenced to the most degrading of all deaths, a torment reserved for men of the lowest social class. To add to the shame, He was to be crucified between two criminals.

He Who took the cross upon His shoulders to carry it for us was Jesus most patient. We, on the other hand, resent sufferings which conflict with our own interests. It is easy for us to give in to feelings of rebellion, and even to really offend God. Let us consider the patient Jesus.

Patience! This is necessary in everything — in prayer life, in work or studies, and in apostolic activities; it is necessary for everyone who wants to live as a human being, a Christian and a religious. It is necessary every hour, every moment. It is patience that makes us saints; if daily we embrace our cross and carry it with Jesus Christ, sharing in His merit, we become saints. Let us carry our cross with patience, as Jesus carried the cross on which He wanted to die: "I have a baptism to be baptized with, and how distressed I am until it is accomplished!" (Lk. 12:50)

What is our estimation of patience? Let us ask it of Mary Most Holy, for she, too, accompanied her Son to Calvary. Let us beg it of Jesus. The Lord generally does not ask great things of us. He asks us to put up with small sufferings which we come across daily — to perform acts of charity and to be faithful to our duties.

Jesus was exhausted. He had not taken any food since the evening before. All night long He had been among the soldiers, who had beaten Him and scoffed at Him. He had suffered much and had lost much blood.

Weak Himself, He was suffering for the weak — for those who allow themselves to be led into sin — for those who consent to sin without resisting their passions, without fighting their doubts, without curbing their affections or without watching their words — for those who fail to renounce evil thought and actions.

We must fight temptations which attract us, as well as those which discourage us or place us in an occasion of being weakened. In temptation, discouragement and discomfort of soul, especially when in danger of falling into a tepid state, let us turn to our Savior, asking Him — in view of the merit of His sufferings — to give us the strength we need.

# "Always Bearing About the Dying of Jesus" — 1

And as they led him away, they laid hold of a certain Simon of Cyrene, coming from the country, and upon him they laid the cross to bear it after Jesus.

Now there was following him a great crowd of people, and of women, who were bewailing and lamenting him. But Jesus turning to them said, "Daughters of Jerusalem, do not weep for me, but weep for yourselves and for your children. For behold, days are coming in which men will say, 'Blessed are the barren, and the wombs that never bore, and breasts that never nursed.' Then they will begin to say to the mountains, 'Fall upon us,' and to the hills, 'Cover us!' For if in the case of green wood they do these things, what is to happen in the case of the dry?" Now there were also two other malefactors led to execution with him. And they came to the place called Golgotha, that is, the Place of the Skull.

And they gave him wine to drink mixed with gall; but when he had tasted it, he would not drink. Then they crucified him there, and the robbers, one on his right hand and the other on his left. And Jesus said, "Father, forgive them, for they do not know what they are doing." Now in dividing his garments, they cast lots.

And the people stood looking on; and the rulers with them kept sneering at him, saying, "He saved others; let him save himself, if he is the Christ, the chosen one of God." And the soldiers also mocked him, coming to him and offering him common wine, and saying, "If you are the King of the Jews, save yourself!"

And Pilate also wrote an inscription and had it put on the cross. And there was written, JESUS OF NAZARETH, THE KING OF THE JEWS. Many of the Jews therefore read this inscription, because the place where Jesus was crucified was near the city; and it was written in Hebrew, in Greek and in Latin. The chief priests of the Jews said therefore to Pilate, "Do not write, 'The king of the Jews,' but, 'He said, I am the King of the Jews.'" Pilate answered, "What I have written, I have written."

Now one of those robbers who were hanged was abusing him, saying, "If you are the Christ, save yourself and us!" But the other in answer rebuked him and said, "Do not even you fear God, seeing that you are under the same sentence? And we indeed justly, for we are receiving what our deeds deserved; but this man has done nothing wrong." And he said to Jesus, "Lord, remember me when you come into your kingdom." And Jesus said to him, "Amen I say to you, this day you shall be with me in paradise."

Now there were standing by the cross of Jesus his mother and his mother's sister, Mary of Cleophas, and Mary Magdelene. When Jesus, therefore, saw his mother and the disciple standing by, whom he loved, he said to his mother, "Woman, behold, your son." Then he said to the disciple, "Behold, your mother." And from that hour the disciple took her into his home. (Mt.

Mt. 27:33-44; Mk. 22-32; Lk. 23:26-43; Jn. 19:17-27

Jesus was exhausted. Not out of compassion for Him—but fearing that He might die before reaching Calvary where they desired to inflict the supreme humiliation upon Him and sing victory around His cross—His enemies forced a certain passerby to help Him.

The two of them carried the cross: Jesus out of love and the Cyrenean because of force.

Yet scarcely had the Cyrenean put his shoulder under the cross, when he felt himself filled with vigor, strength and consolation. Grace entered into him, for all those who consoled Jesus in His passion were in turn consoled by Him.

Let us ask ourselves whether we carry our own cross out of love or out of force. Are we able to suffer something without telling everyone about it? When a soul not only knows how to suffer but suffers willingly and with a serene face, then this soul has drawn near to perfection, or at least has made great strides on the road to perfection.

From the Cyrenean we can learn that when we shall submit to the cross, we shall be consoled and flooded with grace; in fact, there is no penance which is not accompanied by an outpouring of the Holy Spirit. Jesus Christ does not abandon the soul in mortification or in privation, but infuses the Holy Spirit therein more abundantly.

He who mortifies himself makes much spiritual progress. There is no better road to progress than that of self-crucifixion; there is no better means to happiness than that of mortification. There is no greater mission than that of self-immolation and penance.

Pope John XXIII recommended in *Poenitentiam Agere:* "The first exterior penance that all of us must practice is that of accepting from God, with a resigned and trusting spirit, all the sorrows and sufferings that we encounter in life and that which involves effort and inconvenience in fulfilling the obligations of our condition in our daily life and in the practice of Christian virtues."

And he continued: "In addition to the penance which we must necessarily face because of the inevitable sorrows of this mortal life, Christians must be generous enough to offer also to God voluntary mortifications in the imitation of our Divine Redeemer Who, according to the Prince of the Apostles, 'died also once for sins, the Just for the unjust, that he might bring us to God.'"

Such penance is our duty. "It is important to impress on the minds of the faithful," states the *Constitution on the Sacred Liturgy,* "not only the social consequences of sin but also that essence of the virtue of penance which leads to the detestation of sin as an offense against God; the role of the Church in penitential practices is not to be passed over, and the people must be exhorted to pray for sinners."

Let us ask in a special way the graces: to be capable of suffering something, to bear whatever little pain we may encounter during life, and to value interior mortification highly.

Interior mortification has many implications. The mind is to be mortified. We should not abandon ourselves to any thoughts whatsoever, but should nourish only those which are good, not allowing the mind to ramble here and there undisciplined. Mortification should be exercised in regard to reading also.

The mind tends to flee, and should be curbed. If distractions in prayer persist, the mind should be called back repeatedly until the prayer has been concluded.

A prayer in which the soul has fought continually against distractions, in order to stir up at least some sentiments of faith, humility and love, is always a prayer well made, even if it costs much effort.

Mortification is especially to be practiced when one's thoughts are not good—when they are contrary to faith, charity, obedience, patience, purity, and humility. The mind should be recalled to its place and an act of virtue elicited opposed to the temptation—pride countered with an act of humility, impatience with an act of patience, doubt with an act of faith, and so on.

The will, too, must be mortified. Not everything that pleases God, pleases us. Many times our natural tendency is contrary, because always: "The flesh lusts against the spirit" (Gal. 5:17). We have two inclinations: one celestial, which leads us to follow Jesus and Mary; and another, which leads afar, toward freedom—not that freedom enjoyed by the children of God but rather the freedom with which one rebels against God and follows the enticements of the Evil One. To oppose this inclination, an act of obedience is necessary: *not my will but*

*Your will be done.* How much merit there is in this!

Let us see, if in fulfilling our daily obligations we declare continually, and in deed: *May Your will be done on earth as the angels do it in heaven.*

This is a petition of the *Our Father,* and we must always stress it: *Thy will be done on earth as it is in heaven,* and with that diligence and love with which the divine will should be fulfilled.

Interior mortification also includes control of the heart. "Learn from me for I am meek and humble of heart" (Mt. 11:29). Anger and rancor are to be restrained, and sentiments of devotion and love for prayer fostered. A languid, tepid heart does not please the Lord. What does the Eucharistic Christ behold when He approaches at Communion time? Does He see hearts filled with sentiments of devotion, faith and affection, or hearts cold, languid and indifferent to His saving love?

The heart has to be mortified when its tendencies are not right. Let us learn to keep it under control, meanwhile fostering sentiments of faith, generosity, piety, and humility.

In tears and sorrow, the holy women met Jesus at a bend in the road, and He paused to tell them: "Do not weep for me, but weep for

yourselves and for your children" (Lk. 23:28).
Sometimes compassion for the Savior may be
sterile sentimentality, whereas we should
rather weep for the cause of His passion, our
sins. The passion must make us lay bare the
malice of our transgressions.

"Cry for your children," Jesus told the
women, thus reminding us that we must repent for the sins which others might have committed because of us; just as those mothers
would have been responsible for the sins of
their children, had they neglected to give them
a good upbringing.

Woe to those who give scandal.

Scandal is given directly when wrong is
done in front of someone younger, who is thus
encouraged to do evil. When one says malicious
words which disturb a soul, and worse yet,
if one would do this deliberately to ruin a soul
and to induce it to do evil by following his own
sinful path—this would be diabolical scandal.

Indirect scandal is given by every song
sung, every book offered, every criticism
spoken, which brings about sinful suggestion
in the soul of another. The more delicate the
virtue offended, the more serious the scandal.
Indirect scandal is given, for example, when
those who have the power and responsibility
to check abuses do not do so. Those, too, who

are in charge of youth and do not speak out soon enough to indicate what is to be avoided in order to remain upright and good — will be held responsible for their silence!

We must walk with bowed head, for we do not know how far the consequences of our bad examples extend. Who knows what we shall see on the Day of Judgment? How many more souls might have been saved if we had been, perhaps, more zealous!

Let us have true sorrow for our sins, and for those which others have committed because of us.

Let us pray with the liturgy: "Look with favor upon this sacrifice, O Lord. We seek forgiveness of our sins; let us not be burdened with the sins of others. Through Jesus Christ, your Son, our Lord...."

# "Always Bearing About the Dying of Jesus" — 2

Jesus arrived at the place of execution, where the altar of the cross was to be erected for the immolation of the divine Victim.

Scarcely had they reached Calvary when the cortege of soldiers removed the cross from His shoulders and placed it on the ground. Then, with great haste, they laid violent hands on Jesus and stripped Him of His garments.

Meek as a lamb, the Savior let Himself be led, like a victim going to its immolation without complaint. He suffered the contemptible treatment of the soldiers without opening His mouth.

They offered Him gall mixed with myrrh — a drink given to the condemned to alleviate their pain and almost numb the senses. Jesus tasted its bitterness, but would not drink it. He wanted to feel His pain and make the offering of His life consciously in order completely to accomplish the Father's will, and to gain the greatest merit for us.

Let us contemplate Jesus, thus stripped of His garments and tormented. Have we never indulged in vanity in dress? Never indulged in gluttony? Jesus, stripped and given gall and myrrh to drink, atoned for our sins of immodesty and gluttony. Let us strip ourselves of all affections for human and worldly things, that we may please Jesus alone and make reparation for sins of immodesty in dress, gluttony in food, and intemperance in drink.

The cross had been placed on the ground and the Most Patient was now ordered to stretch Himself out upon it. Obedient unto death, Jesus knelt and willingly stretched Himself out.

The executioner raised the hammer, positioned a spike, and struck with violence. The spike ripped through flesh and sinew and was driven into the wood of the cross. Another was driven through the other wrist, and a third into the feet.

What heart is not softened by this sight?

The cross was raised and dropped into place; a murmur of satisfaction arose from the throng. And Jesus exclaimed: "Father, forgive them, for they do not know what they are doing" (Lk. 23:34).

The Savior was now accomplishing the great mystery of reconciliation, offering His blood to the Heavenly Father, imploring the salvation of the sinners for whom He had come into the world.

Shortly thereafter He uttered another word of pardon: "This day you shall be with me in paradise" (Lk. 23:43). The good thief had made a profession of faith in the divinity of Jesus Christ, and therefore received from Him the great promise of paradise. Thus did the Savior begin to apply the fruits of the Redemption to the first repentant sinner.

When a person confesses his sins well and makes the resolution of not falling again, he should no longer be disturbed; rather he should have great confidence in Jesus, our Savior, Who always forgives. We should have truly great confidence in His mercy.

"Woman, behold your Son....behold your Mother" (Jn. 19:26, 27). Each one of us can imagine this word addressed to himself (cf. Pope Paul VI, *The Great Sign*). The *Dogmatic Constitution on the Church* sums up Mary's role in our Redemption thus:

"Predestined from eternity by that decree of divine providence which determined the

*He suffered*
*the contemptible treatment*
*of the soldiers*
*without opening His mouth.*

incarnation of the Word, to be the Mother of God, the Blessed Virgin was on this earth the virgin Mother of the Redeemer, and above all others and in a singular way the generous associate and humble handmaid of the Lord. She conceived, brought forth, and nourished Christ, she presented Him to the Father in the temple, and was united with Him by compassion as He died on the cross. In this singular way she cooperated by her obedience, faith, hope and burning charity in the work of the Savior in giving back supernatural life to souls. Wherefore she is our mother in the order of grace.

"This maternity of Mary in the order of grace began with the consent which she gave in faith at the Annunciation and which she sustained without wavering beneath the cross, and lasts until the eternal fulfillment of all the elect. Taken up to heaven she did not lay aside this salvific duty, but by her constant intercession continued to bring us the gifts of eternal salvation. This however, is to be so understood that it neither takes away from nor adds anything to the dignity and efficaciousness of Christ the one Mediator."

Do we love Mary, consider her as our Mother and place our filial trust in her? Without devotion to Mary, life becomes arid, but with Mary prayer life is more alive, tasks are easier, sacrifices grow pleasant, life is spent holily and one's apostolate bears fruit.

There were two altars on Calvary: one, the cross of Jesus and the other, the heart of Mary, whose soul was pierced by a sword of sorrow while the nails pierced the hands and feet of her Son, Jesus.

The nature of the Blessed Virgin's role in the economy of salvation is clarified in the *Dogmatic Constitution on the Church:* "The maternal duty of Mary toward men in no wise obscures or diminishes the unique mediation of Christ, but rather shows His power. For all the salvific influence of the Blessed Virgin on men originates, not from some inner necessity, but from the divine pleasure. It flows forth from the superabundance of the merits of Christ, rests on His mediation, depends entirely on it and draws all its power from it. In no way does it impede, but rather does it foster the immediate union of the faithful with Christ."

The passion of Jesus and Mary on Calvary was universal; that is, they suffered for the redemption of the world, on behalf of all men.

It is also our duty to make reparation for the sins of humanity and ask the Lord the grace that men will choose the way that leads to the eternal joy of heaven, even if the road be more difficult than the road of pleasure because it is arduous and sometimes strewn with thorns. Pleasure and duty have two very diverse effects. Pleasure presents itself as attractive and alluring; duty, instead, appears as hard and calling for sacrifice. "If anyone wishes to come after me, let him deny himself, and take up his cross daily, and follow me" (Lk. 9:23).

Our passion is universal in its intention, when we suffer to aid the weak, and do penance for all those that are on the way of error, in order to obtain their repentance.

In *Poenitentiam Agere*, Pope John reminded us: "Since each one of us can state together with St. Paul the Apostle: 'I rejoice in the sufferings I bear...and what is lacking of the sufferings of Christ I fill up in my flesh for his body, which is the Church,' we too must be glad that we can offer our sufferings to God 'for the building up of the body of Christ' which is the Church. We must feel ourselves indeed all the more happy and honored that we are called upon to participate in this redeeming of poor humanity which is too often drawn away from the honest road of truth and virtue."

Holiness consists in crucifying ourselves — our wants, whims, will, passions, and desires — for love of Jesus Christ. One who makes prayer life sentimental, is not of Jesus; to be His, one must crucify himself—mortifying his senses, curbing his tongue and placing himself at the service of God in daily life; there is no other way. The resurrection follows a Calvary, and he who only passes around the Calvary, fools himself.

"In all things," wrote St. Paul the Apostle, "we suffer tribulation, but we are not distressed; we are sore pressed, but we are not destitute; we endure persecution but we are not forsaken; we are cast down, but we do not perish; always bearing about in our body the dying of Jesus, so that the life also of Jesus may be made manifest in our bodily frame. For we the living are constantly being handed over to death for Jesus' sake, that the life also of Jesus may be made manifest in our mortal flesh....Even though our outer man is decaying, yet our inner man is being renewed day by day. For our present light affliction, which is for the moment, prepares for us an eternal weight of glory, that is beyond all measure" (2 Cor. 4:8-11; 16-17).

Let us see if there is something within us which should be crucified; let us take up the nails and hammer.

# Placing Ourselves
# with Him
# in the Hands
# of the Father — 1

Now from the sixth hour there was darkness over the whole land until the ninth hour. Jesus, knowing that all things were accomplished, that the Scripture might be fulfilled, said, "I thirst." And at the ninth hour Jesus cried out with a loud voice saying, "Eloi, Eloi, lama sabacthani?" which, translated, is "My God, my God, why have you forsaken me?" And some of the by-standers on hearing this said, "Behold, he is calling Elia." And immediately one of them ran and taking a sponge soaked it in common wine, put it on a reed and offered it to him to drink. But the rest said, "Wait, let us see whether Elia is coming to save him." Therefore, when Jesus had taken the wine, he said, "It is consummated!" And the sun was darkened, and the curtain of the temple was torn in the middle. And Jesus cried out with a loud voice and said, "Father, into your hands I commend my spirit." And having said this, he expired. (Mt. 27:45-50; Mk.
(Mt. 27:45-50; Mk. 15:33-37; Lk. 23:44-46; Jn. 19:28-30).

Jesus' agony on the cross was about to be concluded. In this final period of His life, the Savior manifested the most sublime virtue and consummate perfection.

The life of Christ had followed a course like that of the sun, which when appearing on the horizon, seems to approach almost timidly, but little by little rises and becomes steadily brighter and warmer. He had been born in silence and obscurity: "For when peaceful stillness compassed everything and the night in its swift course was half-spent, your all-powerful word from heaven's royal throne bounded, a fierce warrior into the doomed land" (Wis. 18:14-15). His soul had been penetrated always more by the Holy Spirit: "Jesus advanced in wisdom and age and grace before God and men" (Lk. 2:52).

Jesus Christ immolated Himself through pure love of God. This summit of perfection is manifested in the last words which He pronounced from the cross: "I thirst" (Jn. 19:28); "My God, my God, why have you forsaken me?" (Mk. 15:34); "Father, into your hands I commend my spirit" (Lk. 23:46); and: "It is consummated!" (Jn. 19:30).

"I thirst" (Jn. 19:28). The thirst of Jesus was twofold: material and spiritual.

Anyone with an apostolic spirit feels the thirst for souls. The apostle has two aspirations: souls and the sanctification of souls. He desires the salvation of all, that the kingdom of God may be established over the entire earth.

Therefore, in the Masses at which he assists, in his Communions and visits to the Most Blessed Sacrament, the apostle always asks the salvation of everyone: sinners, separated brethren and non-Christians; he carries them all in his heart.

The holy torment of the apostolic soul is to reach those who are going lost. He wants to plant the cross everywhere, on every coast and in every land: "Give me souls!"

There is a shortage of apostolic hearts, of ministers of God with the true spirit. Let us form a union of prayer and work for the necessary vocations to all forms of the Christian apostolate.

Jesus had suffered abandonment in the Garden, but even more difficult to bear was His abandonment by the Father as He hung from the cross. Until that last moment He had gazed beyond the merciless obstinacy of His enemies to behold the face of the Father, serenely approving.

But at this point the heavens appeared to cloud over; the triumph of His adversaries

seemed complete. Desolating in the extreme
was the spectacle of many souls falling into
hell, notwithstanding His passion. From His
lips arose the cry: "Eloi, Eloi, lama sabacthani?" — that is: "My God, my God, why have
you forsaken me?" (Mt. 27:46)

This mysterious abandonment must be
rightly understood. It refers to the privation
of defense and protection; the Father had
abandoned Jesus to the blind anger of men and
of hell, that protection of which He had spoken:
"And he who sent me is with me; he has not
left me alone, because I do always the things
that are pleasing to him" (Jn. 8:29).

God could have defended His Christ and
impeded the passion in many ways, but the
Most Blessed Trinity had willed that violence
prevail for that hour.

It was not a separation from the Father's
grace and friendship which Jesus spoke of
when He exclaimed: "My God, my God, why
have you forsaken me?" Rather, He referred
to the fact that the Father would not prevent
His death and would not comfort Him in His
spasms of body and spirit. Jesus Christ wanted
to reveal to us how high was the price with
which He redeemed us, how painful was His
death, and with what anguish He could try
those who wish to follow Him. "He who says

that he abides in him, ought himself also to walk just as he walked" (1 Jn. 2:6).

This word of Jesus, then, was not an accusation against God, a complaint or expression of disgust; it was a word most fitting to bring us to understand the magnitude of His sufferings — a confession of the intense pain that He endured for the Father and for souls.

St. Leo explains: "This was not a word of complaint, but of doctrine, telling us that Christ, had chosen to suffer without comfort. He suffered so much that He seemed not to be the Son of God, but a real sinner; He had to make us understand that He atoned for all sins, even the most internal. He declared Himself abandoned (stricken by God) so that we would know that although the martyrs felt some consolation and comfort in their pains, Christ instead was deprived of these and subjected to His torments as completely as was possible."

It was a lament which stirs us to comprehension and compassion, unless we have hearts of stone.

Jesus asked the Father: "Why have you forsaken me?" (Mt. 27:46), not because He was unaware of the motives, for He knew all things, but since we do not know them, He wants us to inquire into them, "so that we might realize the malice of sin...the great evil of damnation...the value of grace...the supreme good of heaven...and the great love and obedience of the Son toward the Father," as St. Robert Bellarmine tells us.

Very instructive are the words of Cornelius a'Lapidé: "Jesus was abandoned so that we might never be abandoned; He was abandoned to liberate us from sin and from hell; He was abandoned in order to speak to us the word of saving love and to reveal the justice and mercy of God—in order to heal our hearts and leave an example of patient suffering. He points out to us the way to heaven, a way difficult and arduous; however, by going before us, He gives us courage. He wants us to consider to what extent we should love Him, so that we will attain to the point of being able to exclaim with St. Paul: 'Who shall separate us from the love of Christ?... These things we overcome because of him who has loved us' (Rom. 8:35, 37).

"Jesus taught us that we should *pray* in sufferings, rather than cease to pray. He Himself prayed in Gethsemane and on the cross, since prayer is strength in difficulty, alleviation for the sick, and help for the weak; it is the pledge and sign of eternal predestination."

This word of Jesus on the cross is of comfort to those many souls who silently suffer a true martyrdom. Jesus wanted to set an example for us in this also. From the agony of Gethsemane "He began to feel dread and to be exceedingly troubled" (Mk. 14:33). Let souls who suffer thus not become discouraged, for their affliction is not a sign of being separated from God. Rather, God wants them wholly for Himself and purifies them; He desires them to be totally crucified with Him, even in regard to their interior faculties.

The more the Lord increases our sufferings, the more occasions He gives us for sanctifying ourselves. Ah, we have not yet plumbed the depths; we have not yet endured what many of the saints endured! The more we resemble Jesus Christ, the more we will share in His glory.

Let us pray, therefore: *Lord Jesus Christ, who being nailed to the cross, with a loud cry and tears prayed to the Father, grant me the grace of always having recourse to You in every tribulation and temptation. Never permit me to be abandoned by Your mercy. From heaven, listen to my pleas, so that in every pain I will know how to acquire merit. I know that You alone are able to save me; I do not trust in others nor in any human means; You alone are Lord, the Most High, Goodness itself. Let my cry come to You, my God, You Who always hear those who humble themselves to beg Your mercy.*

# Placing Ourselves
with Him
in the Hands
of the Father  — 2

"It is consummated" (Jn. 19:30), Jesus exclaimed. *My mission has been completed. All the prophecies were to have been fulfilled in Me; I was to redeem the world with the passion; I was to give the Father infinite glory; I was to establish the Church, to institute the sacraments, to leave a Gospel of salvation, to inaugurate the new sacrifice — and now, everything is accomplished!*

Do *we* live in such a way as to fulfill our entire mission?

The Divine Artist is marvelous not only in the structuring of the whole system of the cosmos, but also in the formation of the smallest flower. There are no two sets of features perfectly alike; so, too, there are no two souls exactly alike. God has special plans for every soul in time and in eternity; and to that end He has provided gifts of nature and grace.

If daily we live according to God's intention and designs, we will be able to exclaim as we look back at the point of death: "It is consummated!" *Lord, what You wanted of me, I have done: I have corresponded to my vocation in life; I have done Your will!* It will be a real consolation, a pledge of paradise. But we must do this in life in order to have such a comfort in death. Then in heaven we will continue to carry out the very same mission.

Then "Jesus cried out with a loud voice and said, 'Father, into your hands I commend my spirit'" (Lk. 23:46).

Having fulfilled the will of the Father, the Savior placed Himself in the hands of God, the just Rewarder Who will recompense everything, even a glass of water given for love of Him.

After saying these words, Jesus bowed His head and expired.

The sacrifice was complete; the world was redeemed: "for it has pleased God the Father that through him, he should reconcile to himself all things, whether on the earth or in the heavens, making peace through the blood of his cross" (Col. 1:20).

Let us become accustomed to consider the crucifixion as present to us daily on the Altar where the Sacrifice of the Cross is perpetually renewed—the sacrifice which is not only an historical fact, but a reality continuing through time and space.

The Mass has the same end and the same merit as the Sacrifice of the Cross, because the victim and the principal offerer of both are the same: Jesus Christ.

"The Mass, the Lord's Supper," explains the *Instruction on the Worship of the Eucharistic Mystery*, "is at the same time and inseparably: a sacrifice in which the Sacrifice of the Cross is perpetuated; a memorial of the death and resurrection of the Lord, Who said 'do this in memory of me' (Lk. 22:19); and a sacred banquet in which, through the communion of the Body and Blood of the Lord, the People of God share the benefits of the Paschal Sacrifice, renew the New Covenant which God has made with man once for all through the Blood of Christ, and in faith and hope foreshadow and anticipate the eschatological banquet in the kingdom of the Father, proclaiming the Lord's death 'till His coming.'" The document continues: "Christ perpetuates in an unbloody manner the Sacrifice offered on the Cross, offering Himself to the Father for the world's salvation through the ministry of priests. The Church, the Spouse and minister of Christ, performs together with Him the role

*"It has pleased God the Father
that through him, he should
reconcile to himself all things,
whether on the earth or the heavens,
making peace through the blood
of his cross" (Col. 1:20).*

of priest and victim, offers Him to the Father and at the same time makes a total offering of herself together with Him."

Let us have great devotion to the Holy Mass and assist at it as often as possible, uniting ourselves to all the priests celebrating Mass all over the earth.

In the liturgical service which takes place on Good Friday, there are four parts: the reading, the solemn prayers, the veneration of the Holy Cross, and Holy Communion. All of these are ordered to one end: to present for our consideration the first dimension of the Paschal Mystery, which is death—the death of Jesus on the cross and our own death to sin; that is, the putting to death of sin.

The cross is raised on high before the gaze of the world. The prophecy is fulfilled: "And I, if I be lifted up from the earth, will draw all things to myself" (Jn. 12:32). Jesus Christ wins souls not with physical might, but with the power of His saving love. And the supreme act of His love is this: "Greater love than this no one has, that one lay down his life for his friends" (Jn. 15:13).

As is sung in the liturgy, "God reigns from a tree." Thus Jesus reigns with His redemptive love—a love which drew Him down to the earth to make Himself man, master, priest and victim

—a love with which He forgives sins and wills to satisfy for our debts to God. The shepherd gives His life to save His sheep.

The Good Friday readings consist of prophecies pointing to the divine sacrifice. From the prophecy of Osee is read: "He has struck us, but he will bind our wounds; he will revive us after two days; on the third day he will raise us up, to live in his presence." This signifies that the Lord calls sinners to repentance, and in repentance to resurrection from evil.

Then is read a passage from Exodus, describing the ceremony with which the paschal lamb was sacrificed. That lamb was a type of the Lamb of God, the Son of God made man — Who went to His death without any resistance, Who went willingly for love of us.

And then the Passion is chanted, showing that the prophecies have been fulfilled in the Person of Jesus Christ.

In the same liturgy, after having reflected upon the crucifixion of Jesus, the Church prays for herself, for the Pope, for bishops, priests and deacons; for all who as yet do not believe; for those who find themselves in material distress; for our separated brethren; and for the Jews, that one day they may acknowledge the Messias.

In the third part of the Good Friday service the cross is solemnly venerated with the kissing of the feet of Jesus — those wounds by which we were redeemed — thus expressing love and gratitude and especially the resolution never more to sin.

The service is concluded with Holy Communion. On that day the bread and wine are not consecrated; pre-consecrated hosts are consumed, for it is the Church's desire that on Good Friday, when the cross is lifted up on Calvary, all may gaze upon it: "in which is our salvation, life and resurrection."

We have contributed to Jesus' death. Let us bow our heads and resolve: No more sin.

# Brief Sufferings
and
Eternal Bliss

Now after these things Joseph of Arimathea, because he was a disciple of Jesus (although for fear of the Jews a secret one), besought Pilate that he might take away the body of Jesus. And Pilate gave permission. He came, therefore, and took away the body of Jesus. And there also came Nicodemus (who at first had come to Jesus by night) bringing a mixture of myrrh and aloes, in weight about a hundred pounds. They therefore took the body of Jesus and wrapped it in linen cloths with the spices, after the Jewish manner of preparing for burial. Now in the place where he was crucified there was a garden, and in the garden a new tomb in which no one had yet been laid. There accordingly, because of the Preparation Day of the Jews, for the tomb was close at hand, they laid Jesus.

Mt. 27:57-66; Mk. 15:42-47;Lk. 23:49-56; Jn. 19:38-42

"I will pour out on the house of David and on the inhabitants of Jerusalem a spirit of grace and petition; and they shall look on him whom they have pierced, and they shall mourn for him as one mourns for an only son, and they shall grieve over him as one grieves over a first-born" (Zach. 12:10).

Let us gaze on the divine Savior, Who has expired on the cross, and contemplate that scene of sorrow a while longer.

Jesus had been crucified. For three hours He had suffered in agony on the hard wood, also enduring internally a torment that no one else could have understood—an agony of heart and spirit.

Jesus Christ died for our salvation—because of our sins. Let us ask of the Lord the grace of a good death, that it may be the crown of our life; we should ask this often.

Let us ask the grace to die after we have had a true interior conversion; after we have corrected our bad habits and habitual defects, or at least after reducing their malice and number to the minimum, and after making satisfaction for the punishment due to them. Let us ask to die in fervor; that is, in an act of ardent love, in a state of intense charity towards the Lord, so that we may love Him intensely throughout eternity. Let us ask to die after having corresponded so faithfully to our vocation in life that we will be able to say: "I have done what the Lord wished of me; I have accomplished His will." If substantially we have accomplished the will of God, despite the imperfections of weakness, then we will have the reward.

Jesus was then taken down from the cross by Joseph of Arimathea and Nicodemus with the help of John and the holy women — and was placed in the arms of the Most Holy Virgin.

Mary contemplated the head, crowned with thorns; the chest, reduced to one wound; the pierced hands.... In that body she read the story of the passion and sorrows of the Savior. Who could express the grief and sacrifice of this afflicted Mother?

What do we think the Virgin would have said? Did she lay blame on Jesus' crucifiers or the scribes and pharisees who had pressed for the death of her Son?

She had had but one word to say throughout her life: *yes*. And she repeated it still on Calvary: *Behold the handmaid of the Lord; may it be done unto me according to His will, as it pleases Him.*

The Holy Virgin had always said *yes* to the Lord in every circumstance, joyous or sorrowful. She had said *yes* when she left her parents, whom she loved very much, to reside in the temple of Jerusalem. She had said *yes* when she was espoused to St. Joseph, since God had wanted her virginity to be publicly guarded and preserved. She had said *yes* when she accepted the divine motherhood. She had said it before Simeon, when she had to flee into Egypt, at Nazareth, when Jesus left her to begin His public life, when she knew that He had been bound and brought before the tribunal, and when He ascended Calvary. And behold the most painful *yes* that she said after He was taken down from the cross: *It is pleasing to the Lord; it is pleasing also to me.*

Declares Pope Paul in his letter, *The Great Sign:*

"Let us recognize the 'goodness and the love of God the Savior,' who, condescending to our misery, so remote from his infinite sanctity, wished to make it easier for us to imitate it by giving us as a model the human person of his mother. She, in fact, among human beings, offers the most shining example and the closest to us, of that perfect obedience whereby we lovingly and readily conform with the will of the eternal Father. Christ himself, as we well know, made this full closeness to the approval of the Father, the supreme ideal of his human behavior, declaring: 'I do always the things that are pleasing to him.'"

Do we have these habitual dispositions, this internal preparation to do the will of God at all times, so that God may do with us whatever He pleases, without finding resistance in our heart, in our life, in our will?

If we are already prepared to say our *yes* to the Lord, then when the time comes we will say, with generosity, joy and great faith: "the will of God be done." When such an internal disposition is lacking, when one loves his own will and is attached to his own opinions, then, when confronted with the will of God, he feels repugnance and adapts himself unwillingly, out of force. But God repays only what is done in accordance with His will; then, and only then, the merit is very great.

How are our interior dispositions? Are we well disposed in everything, or do we have preferences?

Let us examine ourselves on the following points: Am I disposed to accept sickness as well as health? A life long or short? Criticism or praise? Am I disposed to accept and perform always and even joyfully those tasks which are more humiliating, which require greater mortification? Do I consider myself a true servant of God? This is how the Blessed Virgin considered herself—a handmaid of God....

The entire life of Mary was a martyrdom. In a Marian hymn, her chief sorrows are recalled thus:

*"And they shall mourn for him
as one mourns for an only son,
and they shall grieve over him
as one grieves over a first-born"*
(Zach. 12:10).

Remember, Virgin Mary, the sword of sorrow that pierced your heart when the prophecy of Simeon predicted the death of Jesus, your Son—and place in our hearts sorrow for our sins, whereby this sword will slay the Evil One.

Remember, Virgin Mary, the sorrow that you felt when you had to flee with your Son into Egypt. Now, make us, your exiled children, turn from the darkness to the light—to the splendors of the eternal fatherland.

Remember, Virgin Mary, the sorrow that pierced you when you sought Jesus for three days and found Him in the temple. Grant that we may long for Christ and seek Him always and everywhere; crown our search with success.

Remember, Virgin Mary, the sorrow that you experienced when Jesus was captured and bound, scourged and crowned with thorns. Listen, O Mary, to the cry of your children and break the bonds of our sins.

Remember, Virgin Mary, the sorrow you felt when Jesus was raised up on the cross and surrendered His spirit to the Father amid unutterable spasms. Grant that we, too, may participate in the Sacrifice of the Cross.

Remember, Virgin Mary, the sorrow that you had when you received into your arms the body of Jesus with a profound sense of compassion. Take us, too, in your arms, O Mother, that we may rejoice forever in your love.

Remember, Virgin Mary, the sorrow you felt when Jesus, wrapped in linen, was placed in the sepulchre. Cleanse our soul with the Most Precious Blood of your Son, and at the final moment of our life, instill in us sentiments of repentance, of faith, of hope and of love, and then open to us the gates of heaven.

In *The Great Sign,* Pope Paul wrote: "In devoutly contemplating Mary the faithful draw from her a stimulus for trusting prayer, a spur to the practice of penance and to the holy fear of God. Likewise, it is in this Marian elevation that they more often hear echoing the words with which Jesus Christ announced the advent of the kingdom of heaven: 'Repent and believe in the Gospel'; and His severe admonition: 'Unless you repent you will all perish in the same manner.'"

Let us ask of Mary, in virtue of her sorrows, that our hearts may become like unto hers and that we may acquire skill in the practice of penance and mortification — a mortification which not only counters evil, but which especially strives to replace evil with good.

Jesus was carried to the sepulchre. Behold the honorable funeral He was given: a new tomb, perfumes for the embalming of His body, a shroud and a face cloth.

Virgin and penitent souls accompanied Him to the tomb: Mary, His Mother, the pious women, John, Joseph of Arimathea and Nicodemus.

They wept on their journey from Calvary to the sepulchre, but theirs were not tears of desolation. They did not weep as if they had no faith nor hope, or as if they believed that they had lost a dear one forever. Tears were shed, but they were enlightened tears; sorrow was alleviated by hope in the resurrection.

It is true that this hope was rather weak in the others, but it was always intense in the Blessed Virgin. She completely understood the mission of Jesus and the prophecies concerning Him. Jesus had predicted His passion and death three times, clearly, and He had always added: "On the third day I will rise again" (cf. Lk. 18:33).

The Blessed Virgin gave courage to the others with her faith and certainty. She did not urge that the embalming be completed. And even on Saturday evening and Sunday morning, when the holy women went in search of spices and perfumes to finish embalming Jesus, Mary did not accompany them, because of her certainty and expectation of the resurrection.

When the Lord appeared, she was waiting for Him, her heart rejoicing fully.

What will our own grave be like? That of Jesus was glorious.

The tomb of Jesus was the place of His triumph. Behold what awaits us. Courage! Because of original sin we are condemned to trial, to death, to the grave, to the corruption of the body, but then: eternal bliss, glory and reward—that is what awaits us. Let us always aim for the reward, always keeping our sights fixed on eternity and paradise, and then we will understand everything: why we must suffer and why pain has to come right into our own lives.

In his inexpressible torment, Job said feelingly: "I know that my Redeemer lives, and... I shall see God" (Job 19:25-26).

And David, unjustly persecuted by Saul, exclaimed in the height of his anguish and the depths of his abandonment: "I believe that I shall see the bounty of the Lord in the land of the living" (Ps. 26:13).

There is a paradise to look forward to, and no suffering is too great in view of the magnitude of the reward. There is no comparison between brief sufferings and eternal bliss.

# Newness of Life in the Lord Jesus

At that time Mary Magdalene, and Mary the mother of James, and Salome, brought spices, that they might go and anoint him. And very early on the first day of the week, they came to the tomb, when the sun had just risen. And they were saying to one another, "Who will roll the stone back from the entrance of the tomb for us?" And looking up they saw that the stone had been rolled back, for it was very large. But on entering the tomb, they saw a young man sitting at the right side, clothed in a white robe, and they were amazed. He said to them, "Do not be terrified. You are looking for Jesus of Nazareth, who was crucified. He has risen, he is not here. Behold the place where they laid him. But go, tell his disciples and Peter, that he goes before you into Galilee; there you shall see him, as he told you. Remember how he spoke to you while he was yet in Galilee, saying that the Son of Man must be betrayed into the hands of sinful men, and be crucified, and on the third day rise."

And they remembered his words. And having returned from the tomb, they reported all these things to the Eleven, and to all the rest.

Mt. 28:1-10; Mk. 16:1-7; Lk. 24:1-9

"And on the third day he rose again.... He will come again in glory to judge the living and the dead, and of his kingdom there will be no end." Let us sing this Creed together with the angels in heaven, who rejoice over the resurrection of Jesus Christ, king of angels and saints.

Several reflections may be made on the Gospel of Easter morning. The first is historical: the fact of the resurrection. The Lord Jesus appeared to Mary Magdalene, to the holy women, to St. Peter, twice to the disciples as they were gathered in the upper room, again to five hundred disciples at once.... These events clearly show the authenticity of the resurrection.

A doctrinal reflection on this passage should lead us to ponder the resurrection more deeply. It is the central and the greatest of the truths foretold by Jesus Christ, and that with which He confirmed His other teachings. Having already conquered sin, Jesus conquered death in the resurrection.

A liturgical reflection shows us Easter as the focal point of all Christian feasts. Those which precede it are preparatory; those which follow it are the consequences and fruit we derive from the mystery of the Lord's resurrection.

There is also a moral reflection which can be made, taken from St. Paul's first letter to the Corinthians: "Brethren: Purge out the old leaven, that you may be a new dough, as you really are without leaven. For Christ, our passover, has been sacrificed. Therefore let us keep festival, not with the old leaven, nor with the leaven of malice and wickedness, but with the unleavened bread of sincerity and truth" (1 Cor. 5:7-8). Let us, then, change our life, rooting and grounding our life in Christ and His life in us: "For me to live is Christ" (Phil. 1:21).

Let us deepen our faith in the resurrection of Jesus Christ, and witness to it before the world: "witnesses of his resurrection" (cf. Acts 1:22). The resurrection is the basis of our salvation. St. Paul invites us to proclaim it with our lips and believe it firmly in our hearts: "If you confess with your mouth that Jesus is the Lord, and believe in your heart that God has raised him from the dead, you shall be saved" (Rom 10:9). Let us give ourselves plentiful assurance of salvation, by settling ourselves on this firm foundation of faith and witness.

We should give the glorious mysteries of the Rosary, especially that of the resurrection, a special place among our devotions. Let us rejoice with the Blessed Virgin, exclaiming: "Queen of heaven, rejoice—alleluia!—for He Whom you have deserved to bear—alleluia!—has risen as He said—alleluia!

In the Second Epistle to Timothy, the last of his letters, St. Paul made this recommendation to his beloved disciple: "Remember that Jesus Christ *rose from the dead*" (2 Tim. 2:8).

The magnificent reality of the resurrection concerns Jesus Christ and the men who will rise with Him. The victory over death is conclusive; death will be no more. "Christ, having risen from the dead, *dies now no more,* death shall no longer have dominion over him. For the death that he died, he died to sin once for all, but the life that he lives, he lives unto God" (Rom. 6:9-10). In a word, the resurrection is the conclusive victory of life.

Contained in the historical fact of the resurrection are further precious realities and sublime ends.

The first of these is the glorification of the Son of God, Who, in obedience to the Father and for the benefit of all His adopted brothers, accepted the most utter ignominy to the point of dying the infamous death of the cross. It is a principle frequently set forth by the Lord Jesus in His preaching: "He who humbles himself shall be exalted" (Lk. 14:11). The resurrection is the eternal exaltation of Jesus Christ before mankind: "He humbled himself, becoming obedient unto death, even to death on a cross. Therefore God also has exalted him" (Phil. 2:8-9).

This magnificent reality of the resurrection also strengthens our faith, which is anchored completely in the resurrection of Christ. All of man's more sublime expectations are rooted in this: "If Christ has not risen, vain is your faith, for you are still in your sins" (1 Cor. 15:17).

The resurrection feeds the flame of human hope, which is the great guarantee of the Christian's imperturbable optimism, and a powerful incentive to the performance of good works to merit the eternal reward in the future resurrection. It is St. Peter who presents this prospect to us in his first letter: "Blessed be the God and Father of our Lord Jesus Christ, who according to his great mercy *has begotten us again, through the resurrection of Jesus Christ from the dead, unto a living hope, unto an incorruptible inheritance — undefiled and unfading,* reserved for you in heaven" (1 Pt. 1:3-4).

The resurrection is the consummation of the Redemption. The mystery of our salvation does not end with the suffering and death of Jesus Christ; its true conclusion is to be found in His resurrection, which offers us the fruit, the perfect consummation: "who was delivered up for our sins, *and rose again for our justification*" (Rom. 4:25).

Finally, the resurrection of Jesus Christ directs our gaze upward, and gives life a new emphasis and intensity. Therefore St. Paul frequently based an emphatic call to live a truly Christian life upon the thought of the resurrection of the Lord Jesus: "Just as Christ has arisen from the dead through the glory of the Father, so may we also walk *in newness of life*" (Rom. 6:4).

Let us also reflect upon the theological truth of the resurrection of the dead. As Jesus Christ rose, so shall we rise. On that great Day we will be called forth from the grave to a new life, the souls of the elect descending from heaven to be united again to their bodies, and the souls of the wretched emerging from hell to be united again to their bodies. But what a difference there will be between them! How ugly will be the bodies of the damned; to vindicate the justice of God, the marks of their sins will be impressed upon them for all to see. For

0. Paschal Mystery

*"Blessed be the God
and Father of our Lord Jesus Christ,
who according to his great mercy
has begotten us again..." (1 Pt. 1:3-4).*

all are to behold how just the Lord is, and how He gives to each what each has merited.

How glorious, instead, will be the bodies of the elect! They will be marked with their good deeds, the virtues they have practiced, and their zeal. The bodies of apostles will be twice as glorious, doubly resplendent—for in addition to doing good themselves these have also taught others to do good. The body of the Lord Jesus is resplendent; His wounds blaze like suns in heaven; and the bodies of the elect will resemble His, for the elect became similar to Jesus Christ in this life.

Let us think about our senses—our hearing, vision, taste, touch, feelings, imagination and memory. Let us think of all our faculties. Each of them will be gratified, if we have truly used them for God, if we have made a real effort to become similar to Jesus Christ and have merited His life.

But what will become of those who have abused their external and internal senses, heart and mind? What will become of them on that solemn Day when each of us will receive the final, eternal sentence—when the Lord Jesus will pass sentence upon everyone in the world who has rejected Him and everyone who has welcomed and followed Him?

Let us especially ask the grace to believe more firmly in our final resurrection and to think more frequently of that solemn Day. What joy for the elect—triumph with Jesus Christ! What bitterness, tears and despair for the lost! Here on earth we are on trial; God leaves us free. But the Day is coming in which He will judge the good and the wicked and give to each as he deserves.

We, however, having chosen to follow Jesus and live according to Him, will have our Easter—our passover from one life to another. Easter (Passover) was symbolized in the journey of the Hebrews from Egypt to the promised land and fulfilled in Christ: "Christ, our passover, has been sacrificed" (1 Cor. 5:7). We have endeavored spiritually to live this passover, passing, in regard to fervor, from one life to another. Let us think of life's value in relation to eternity.

Let us also consider life with regard to the time which is fleeting. Blessed are they who make the most of their opportunities, and unfortunate they who consume their time in sinning or in doing nothing or little.

The words of the Apostle are appropriate: "But if we have died with Christ, we believe that we shall also live together with Christ. Thus do you consider yourselves also as dead to sin, but alive to God in Christ Jesus" (Rom. 6:8, 11).

# With the Lord in His Kingdom

Now he led them out toward Bethany, and he lifted up his hands and blessed them. And it came to pass as he blessed them, that he parted from them and was carried up into heaven. And while they were gazing up to heaven as he went, behold, two men stood by them in white garments, and said to them, "Men of Galilee, why do you stand looking up to heaven? This Jesus who has been taken up from you into heaven, shall come in the same way as you have seen him going up to heaven." And they...returned to Jerusalem with great joy. And they were continually in the temple, praising and blessing God.                                   Lk. 24:50-53; Acts 1:10-11

The Paschal Mystery, in which Jesus Christ redeemed men and gave perfect glory to God through His passion, death and resurrection, was completed in His glorious ascension into heaven.

For forty days after His resurrection, the Lord had appeared repeatedly to the Apostles, giving them very clear proofs that He had risen. Then He again appeared in the Cenacle, where the Apostles were gathered together, ate His last meal with them, and invited them to leave Jerusalem and climb the Mount of Olives, which is the highest of the mountains surrounding the city. There He gave them their final instructions and entrusted to them the mission they were about to undertake. While blessing them, He began to ascend toward the heavens; they were still spellbound when suddenly a cloud hid Him from their view.

We may imagine that in that moment Christ was met by the just of the Old Testament, and that leading them He entered into heaven, where He passed by the angelic choirs to seat Himself at the right hand of His Father.

In celebrating this triumphal reality, the sacred liturgy calls us to rejoicing: "All you peoples, clap your hands, shout to God with cries of gladness" (Ps. 46:2).

The boundless joy of this event has a two-fold source: the triumph of Jesus Christ, Who ascends into heaven to be reunited with the Father after His marvelous human life, and the implication of this event for us — the implication that humanity ascends into heaven in Christ human nature, united to the divine nature in the Person of the Son of God, has made its way through the limitless expanses of the heavens.

The ascension puts the finishing touches on the way which God has shown to man. Jesus Christ, who is the Way to go to the Father—way in example, doctrine, grace, and in His living humanity itself—now shines forth as Way in His marvelous ascension: "ascending on high."

While we glorify the Lord Jesus ascended in splendor, let us revive our faith in our future ascension into heaven. After the resurrection of the dead, body and soul reunited, we, too, will ascend into heaven, if we live now our own paschal mystery, "dying to sin and becoming conformed to Christ," as the *Constitution on the Sacred Liturgy* exhorts us, "that we may live no longer for ourselves but for Him who died for us and rose again" (cf. 2 Cor. 5:15).

So that the Apostles would grasp this significance also, two angels appeared to them while they were still gazing heavenward in wonder, and asked: "Men of Galilee, why do you stand looking up to heaven? This Jesus who has been taken up from you into heaven, shall come in the same way as you have seen him going up to heaven" (Acts 1:11). The angels meant: *Now that you have lived with Jesus for three years, now that you have seen Him ascend into heaven, do what He taught you, carry out the mission He has given you, and then you too, will ascend into heaven. Jesus will return; He will return at the end of the world; He will return to take you, and lead you into the glory which is His.*

Let us enliven our faith in Christ's ascension; this is faith in Christ the Way: *"a new and living way"* (Heb. 10:20). He is the Way linking earth and heaven, rejecting not the earth, but utilizing it for heaven.

Let us reflect that Jesus Christ ascended into heaven because He fulfilled the will of the Father.

Let us reflect, too, that heaven will be the vision, possession and enjoyment of God. Only there will the heart be filled with joy—filled to overflowing—for God is infinite.

So many of our troubles and difficulties would vanish if we gave more thought to eternal life. We would be more fervent, virtuous and zealous.

The thought of eternal life, then, should elicit a threefold response from us: our faith in heaven should increase; our lives should be directed more towards heaven; and we should pray for the graces necessary to merit heaven.

Why are men so preoccupied over the things of this earth? Because they do not reflect that there is a heaven. They forget what a great joy God has prepared for the just. And therefore serious sins are committed, the flesh indulged, ambitions satisfied, and the things of this world prized and coveted. Happiness is sought here, whereas it should be sought beyond. There are Christians who profess their faith in life everlasting in the Creed, but then live as if there were no heaven. They speak like non-believers and seek only the satisfactions of this earth.

Let us pray for an increase of faith in heaven; faith is a gift of God.

Two great truths must not only be believed but "felt": "He who comes to God must believe that God exists and is a rewarder to those who seek him" (Heb. 11:6). God will repay us! Let us work for Him, and thus for ourselves. Let us order our lives towards heaven, thinking, like shrewd businessmen, of the reward awaiting us—the end for which we were created—and directing all our life towards it.

Religious, especially, should think of heaven. With his profession, the religious says: "Here on earth I want nothing. I want only You, Lord. I want heaven." And how can one find good vocations if he does not promise them a reward? One easily gives his life—his all, in fact—to gain the "All"—the Lord!

What instead is the "all" of this earth? "Affliction of spirit," and nothing else.

Why do we work so slowly sometimes? Because we do not reflect upon the great profit we can gain for ourselves by making each moment of life render the maximum. Let us allow the thought of eternal life to dominate us!

Every morning, then, let us remind ourselves of this most consoling truth—heaven. Once we have had sufficient rest, we should awaken ourselves to fervor. If the prayer life of the morning is neglected, the duties of the day will be neglected even more. The secret of the day lies in the spiritual exercises of the early hours. Just as one begins the day, so he can hope to continue and end it.

One arouses himself to fervor chiefly in the preventive examination of conscience: What did I do yesterday? What should I do today? What dangers and temptations will I encounter? This reflection will reinforce our will, but to do so it must be concluded with a firm resolution, especially one made in the light of the last things—death, judgment, heaven and hell.

Two dimensions of the Christian mystery are the mystery of our purification and the

*Let us reflect that heaven
will be the vision, possession
and enjoyment of God.
Only there will the heart
be filled with joy —
filled to overflowing —
for God is infinite.*

mystery of new life, our resurrection in Christ. Purification from every evil is required, so that we may live the new and risen life in Jesus Christ. We are to go against thoughts, feelings, words and deeds springing from corrupt nature; let us seek instead to bear new fruits of holiness: to become similar to Christ and live in Him — not only exteriorly but in such a way that the Father, Who first of all sees our minds and hearts, will find us worthy and similar to His Son.

*The Dogmatic Constitution on the Church* thus emphasizes the universal call to holiness: "The followers of Christ are justified in the Lord Jesus, because in the baptism of faith they truly become sons of God and sharers in the divine nature. In this way they are really made holy. Then too, by God's gift, they must hold on to and complete in their lives this holiness they have received. They are warned by the Apostle to live 'as becomes saints,' and to put on 'as God's chosen ones, holy and beloved, a heart of mercy, kindness, humility, meekness, patience,' and to possess the fruit of the Spirit in holiness."

St. Paul could say: "Indeed I am hard pressed from both sides — desiring to depart and to be with Christ..." (Phil. 1:23). He who had been taken up into heaven to contemplate its beauties, desired to break the bonds which held him to the earth in order to enjoy his ineffable vision.

Let us think of heaven and rejoice. I am working for heaven! I am not working for a hope which can delude me (and certainly one who hopes in earthly goods will be deluded, since he will leave all when he dies). I work "...awaiting the blessed hope and glorious coming of our great God and Savior, Jesus Christ" (Tit. 2:13).

And therefore let us ask for and practice the virtue of hope more intensely, thinking of heaven in difficulties and temptations. And then we will understand the expression of St. Francis of Assisi: "So great is the joy which awaits me that every pain is a delight." The Christian should always be inundated by a great joy and a living fervor. One who thinks little of heaven will soon become tepid. But he who has his eyes on the goal, quickens his steps and does not feel tired — or if he does feel so (and this is human), he loves the very fatigue, and is courageous, fervent and enterprising for his own perfection and for his mission in life.

"If you have risen with Christ," St. Paul exhorts us, "seek the things that are above, where Christ is seated at the right hand of God. Mind the things that are above, not the things that are on earth. For you have died and your life is hidden with Christ in God. When Christ, your life, shall appear, then you too will appear with him in glory" (Col. 3:1-4).

Let us think of heaven. Let us think of it especially when we awaken in the morning: *Today I will work for heaven.*

# The Gift
# of the
# Spirit

And he said to them, "Go into the whole world and preach the gospel to every creature. He who believes and is baptized shall be saved, but he who does not believe shall be condemned."

And while eating with them, he charged them not to depart from Jerusalem, but to wait for the promise of the Father, "of which you have heard," said he, "by my mouth; for John baptized with water, but you shall be baptized with the Holy Spirit not many days hence."

They therefore who had come together began to ask him, saying, "Lord, will you at this time restore the kingdom to Israel?"

But he said to them, "It is not for you to know the times or dates which the Father has fixed by his own authority; but you shall receive power when the Holy Spirit comes upon you, and you shall be witnesses for me in Jerusalem and in all Judea and Samaria and even to the very ends of the earth."

And when he had said this, he was lifted up before their eyes, and a cloud took him out of their sight.

Then they returned to Jerusalem from the mount called Olivet, which is near Jerusalem, a Sabbath day's journey. And when they had entered the city, they mounted to the upper room where were staying Peter and John, James and Andrew, Philip and Thomas, Bartholomew and Matthew, James the son of Alpheus, and Simon the Zealot, and Jude the brother of James. All these with one mind continued steadfastly in prayer with the women and Mary, the mother of Jesus and his brethren.

And when the days of Pentecost were drawing to a close, they were all together in one place. And suddenly there came a sound from heaven, as of a violent wind blowing, and it filled the whole house where they were sitting. And there appeared to them parted tongues as of fire, which settled upon each of them. And they were all filled with the Holy Spirit and began to speak in foreign tongues, even as the Holy Spirit prompted them to speak.

But they went forth and preached everywhere, while the Lord worked with them and confirmed the preaching by the signs that followed. Mk. 16:15-20; Acts 1:4-9, 12-14; 2:1-4

Let us consider the ancient biblical expression which St. Paul applies precisely to the ascension of Christ: "Ascending on high, he led away captives; he gave gifts to men" (Eph. 4:8).

He gave gifts to men. Commenting on this phrase, St. Thomas notes briefly: "gifts of grace and glory." The primary and essential gift for man on his earthly pilgrimage is the gift of the Spirit, Who is defined precisely as Gift: "highest gift of God." But the ascension of Christ into heaven had to take place before His coming: "If I do not go, the Advocate will not come to you" (Jn. 16:7).

This Gift more than sufficiently sums up all of Christ's lavish bestowal at His ascension, confirming His assurance to the Apostles that they would not be left in the world as orphans.

With an intense preparation of ten days, the Church became worthy to receive the Holy Spirit on the day of Pentecost, and since then, she has been receiving Him continuously.

Mary, the Mother of Jesus, led the Apostles in prayer, encouraging them, assisting them to elevate their minds in hope, and recalling for them Christ's promises to send the Holy Spirit.

The Blessed Virgin, who had hastened the descent of God's Son to the earth and who had signalled the hour in which the Incarnate Word should begin His public mission, now entreated the Father to send the Giver of light, the Holy Spirit. She was then exercising her role as Mother of the Church, Mother of the Apostles.

Let us invoke the Holy Spirit with and through Mary. May He descend with His seven gifts, bestowing on us heavenly wisdom, the understanding of things spiritual, counsel, fortitude, knowledge, piety, and holy fear of God.

"Just as Christ was sent by the Father," states the *Constitution on the Sacred Liturgy,* "so also He sent the apostles, filled with the Holy Spirit. This He did that, by preaching the gospel to every creature, they might proclaim that the Son of God, by His death and resurrection, had freed us from the power of Satan and from death, and brought us into the kingdom of His Father. His purpose also was that they might accomplish the work of salvation which they had proclaimed, by means of sacrifice and sacraments, around which the entire liturgical life revolves. Thus by baptism men are plunged into the Paschal Mystery of Christ: they die with Him, are buried with Him, and rise with Him; they receive the spirit of adoption as sons 'in which we cry Abba, Father' (Rom. 8:15), and thus become true adorers whom the Father seeks."

Here the way of the apostolate is pointed out: the mission of saving men is left to man, since this is the will of God, that men save themselves through other men; and all deference and faith should be rendered to those who are called to this office. The priest is to be believed and followed; through him is grace to be received. To the priestly mission are united all those who desire to be associated with it, whether in living a life of individual perfection or in performing an apostolate.

To the Corinthians St. Paul wrote: "I am jealous for you with a divine jealousy" (2 Cor. 11:2). He wanted them all to belong entirely to Christ; his desires and designs for those souls were the same as those of God.

Zeal is born of love, nurtured by love and completed in love. Zeal and love of God are inseparable. For this reason St. Augustine states that one who does not have zeal does not love. It would be wrong for a Christian to want to attend only to himself and not engage in works of zeal.

The Son of God came down from heaven and became incarnate in order to save men who were lost through sin: "Who for us men and for our salvation came down from heaven." He died for us on the cross: "Who gave Himself a ransom for all..." (1 Tim. 2:6).

The Redemption is completed.

The world is redeemed, but if the fruits of the Redemption were not applied to men, what would it avail? The Gospel must be preached. The *Decree on the Mission Activity of the Church* declares:

"Divinely sent to the nations of the world to be unto them 'a universal sacrament of salvation,' the Church, driven by the inner necessity of her own catholicity, and obeying the mandate of her Founder (cf. Mk. 16:16), strives ever to proclaim the Gospel to all men. The Apostles themselves, on whom the Church was founded, following in the footsteps of Christ, 'preached the word of truth and begot churches.' It is the duty of their successors to make this task endure 'so that the word of God may run and be glorified' (2 Thess. 3:1) and the kingdom of God be proclaimed and established throughout the world. In the present state of affairs, out of which there is arising a new situation for mankind, the Church, being the salt of the earth and the light of the world (cf. Mt. 5:13-14), is more urgently called upon to save and renew every creature, that all things may be restored in Christ and all men may constitute one family in Him and one people of God."

Our conclusion should be to help Jesus Christ, with our zeal, to save souls — to bring the Redemption to completion. Christ wants to save men by means of men. In the first place, this is the mission of the priesthood, to whom the Lord said: "Go into the whole world and preach the Gospel to every creature" (Mk. 16:15). In the second place, it is the mission of all religious of apostolic life, and in the third, the mission of the laity.

"The members of the Church," declares the *Decree on the Mission Activity of the Church,* "are impelled to carry on such missionary activity by reason of the love with which they love God and by which they desire to share with all men the spiritual good of both this life and the life to come."

What must we do? We must give Him Whom we have received — Jesus Christ. "For I myself," wrote St. Paul, "have received from the Lord what I also delivered to you..." (1 Cor. 2:23) — the same truth, the same Gospel, the same faith. Thus we must allow no self love whatsoever to creep into our apostolate, in imitation of the Blessed Virgin, who was most humble, and offered Jesus Christ to the world.

The *Dogmatic Constitution on the Church* reminds us: "'God is love, and he who abides in love, abides in God, and God in Him.'" But, God pours out his love into our hearts through the Holy Spirit, Who has been given to us; thus the first and most necessary gift is love, by which we love God above all things and our neighbor because of God. It is the love of God and the love of one's neighbor which points out the true disciple of Christ."

Extremely valuable also is the apostolate of suffering. In fact, it is most necessary and effective. As the same constitution expresses it: "May all those who are weighed down with poverty, infirmity and sickness, as well as those who must bear various hardships or who suffer persecution for justice' sake—may they all know they are united with the suffering Christ in a special way for the salvation of the world."

True zeal is pure—that is, the glory of God, not self-glory is its aim; the salvation of souls, not personal profit, is its goal.

True zeal is extensive, also. It extends to all—to the poor as well as to the workers; to the sinners as well as to the just. As the *Decree on the Mission Activity of the Church* reminds us: "Since this mission goes on and in the course of history unfolds the mission of Christ Himself, who was sent to preach the Gospel to the poor, the Church, prompted by the Holy Spirit, must walk in the same path on which Christ walked: a path of poverty and obedience, of service and self-sacrifice to the death, from which death He came forth a victor by His resurrection. For thus did all the Apostles walk in hope, and by many trials and sufferings they filled up those things wanting to the Passion of Christ for His body which is the Church" (cf. Col. 1:24).

Zeal is strong in trials, difficulties and failures; in bearing ingratitude and overcoming obstacles.

True zeal is also sincere and prudent: that is, one first looks after one's own soul, then uses the proper means at the proper time — keeping in mind the circumstances of times, persons and places.

Zeal conforms itself to the divine Master, Who sought the Apostles, formed them and prayed and suffered for them; He rendered them perfect by sending the Holy Spirit to assist them and confirm their words with miracles. The first and principal concern of every apostle is to seek out and form vocations to the apostolate.

The Lord Jesus said, "I am the light of the world" (Jn. 8:12). After He ceased to preach, the Apostles began to do so, for the Master had also told them: "You are the light of the world" (Mt. 5:14).

# The Daily
# Paschal Mystery  —  1

Jesus, having offered one sacrifice for sins, has taken his seat forever at the right hand of God.... For by one offering he perfected forever those who are sanctified. Thus also the Holy Spirit testifies unto us. For after having said, "This is the covenant that I will make with them after those days, says the Lord: I will put my laws upon their hearts, and upon their minds I will write them," he then adds, "And their sins and iniquities I will remember no more."

Heb. 10:12-17

For I myself have received from the Lord (what I also delivered to you), that the Lord Jesus, on the night he was betrayed, took bread, and giving thanks broke, and said, "This is my body which shall be given up for you; do this in remembrance of me." In like manner also the cup, after he had supped, saying, "This cup is the new covenant in my blood; do this as often as you drink it, in remembrance of me. For as often as you shall eat this bread and drink the cup, you proclaim the death of the Lord, until he comes."

1 Cor. 11:23-26

And they continued steadfastly in the teach-
ing of the apostles and in the communion of the
breaking of the bread and in the prayers.

Acts 2:42

"At your house I am keeping the Passover
with my disciples" (Mt. 26:18). Jesus keeps
the Passover with us, His disciples. Loving us,
He did not will that the sacrifice of His love
be renewed year after year, but rather day by
day.

Every day the Lord renews the Sacrifice
of the Cross to pay for our daily sins. And every
day He invites us: "Take and eat; this is my
body; he who eats my flesh and drinks my
blood has life everlasting" (Mt. 26:26; Jn. 6:55).

"At the Last Supper," states the *Instruction
on the Worship of the Eucharistic Mystery,* "on
the night when he was betrayed, our Savior
instituted the Eucharistic Sacrifice of his
body and blood. He did this in order to perpetuate the Sacrifice of the Cross throughout
the centuries until he should come again, and
so to entrust to his beloved spouse, the Church,
a memorial of his death and resurrection: a
sacrament of love, a sign of unity, a bond of
charity, a paschal banquet in which Christ is
eaten, the mind is filled with grace, and a
pledge of future glory is given to us."

"Christ is present in the Sacrifice of the Mass," declares the *Constitution on the Sacred Liturgy*, "not only in the person of his minister, 'the same now offering, through the ministry of priests, who formerly offered himself on the cross' (Trent), but especially under the eucharistic species."

Jesus Christ offers Himself to the Father in each Mass with a special act of His will — through that same most ardent desire for the glory of God and salvation of men which was His on the cross. "As often as the sacrifice of the cross in which Christ our passover was sacrificed (1 Cor. 5:7) is celebrated on an altar," states the *Constitution on the Church*, "the work of our redemption is carried on."

The differences between the Sacrifice of the Cross and the Sacrifice of the Mass are accidental. On the cross the victim was mortal, passible, visible; in the Mass, instead, He is present in His sacramental state — immortal, impassible, invisible. As Pope Paul wrote in *Mystery of Faith:* "The way Christ is made present in this Sacrament is none other than by the change of the whole substance of the bread into his body, and of the whole substance of the wine into his blood, and this unique and truly wonderful change the Catholic Church rightly calls transubstantiation."

On the cross the Redemption was accomplished; in the Mass it is applied.

The Eucharistic Sacrifice is offered to adore, thank, propitiate and supplicate God.

God is the supreme good; there is nothing good which does not come from Him. He is the source of all, just as He is the destiny of all. Infinite is the number of His perfections, and each perfection is infinite in itself. God needs nothing, for He is utterly happy; yet His love expressed itself in the creation of every being other than Himself.

We, His creatures, therefore, owe Him the gratitude, honor, and adoration He deserves. Yet we cannot render to God an honor proportional to His greatness. This honor only Jesus Christ, true man yet also true God, can give. And this He does in the Holy Mass where He is represented in a state of immolation. This state acknowledges God's supreme dominion over all things; they are for Him alone.

"Through him (Christ), therefore, let us offer up a sacrifice of praise always to God." (Heb. 13:15)

The Mass also has the purpose of thanksgiving—its eucharistic end. All that we have, has come from God: "What have you that you have not received?" (1 Cor. 4:7) Creation, redemption and sanctification are from God.

From Him come life, the soul with its faculties, the body with its senses, and all the blessings showered upon the world, the Church and ourselves: "How shall I make a return to the Lord for all the good he has done for me? The cup of salvation I will take up, and I will call upon the name of the Lord" (Ps. 115:12-13).

Before consecrating the bread, Jesus Christ gave thanks to the Father; before consecrating the wine, He likewise gave thanks. Thus, this sacrifice is eucharistic. What thanksgiving is more worthy than that which is offered to the Father by His Incarnate Son? It has an infinite value; God is pleased with it, as is said in the prayer: "Look with favor upon these offerings. Accept them...."

The Eucharistic Sacrifice is propitiatory. Every time the sacrifice is repeated, the work of our redemption is renewed. Consecrating the bread and wine at the Last Supper, Jesus Christ said of His Body: "which shall be given up for you" (1 Cor. 11:24). Of His Blood, He said: "which shall be shed for you" (Lk. 22:20).

"By means of the Mystery of the Eucharist," writes Pope Paul in *Mystery of Faith*, "the Sacrifice of the Cross, which was once offered on Calvary, is marvelously re-enacted and its saving power is constantly recalled and applied for the forgiveness of those sins which we daily commit."

The purpose of petition is well expressed by the words following the Preface, in which we supplicate the Father: "to accept and bless the gifts we offer you in sacrifice. We offer them for your holy catholic Church. Watch over it and guide it; grant it peace and unity...."

The Mass is the breviary of the Incarnation, life, ministry and Paschal Mystery of Jesus Christ. In this light let us consider its main parts, the liturgy of the Word and the eucharistic liturgy, which are so closely connected that they form one single act of worship.

In the liturgy of the Word, we perceive the divine truths — the food of our minds and substance of our faith. Just as Jesus Christ preached the Good News before offering the Sacrifice of the Cross, so in the Mass the sacrifice is preceded by instruction. The *Constitution on the Sacred Liturgy* declares: "The faithful should be instructed by God's Word."

In the Epistle and Gospel especially is the bread of God's Word to be had, while the Introit and Prayer stress what we should learn and profess. "In the liturgy," states the same document, "God speaks to his people and Christ is still proclaiming his Gospel. And the people reply to God both by song and prayer."

Every Mass has a message, and if this is followed well, the teachings of God are grasped, at least in some degree.

There are yet, however, thoughts which are not the thoughts of Jesus Christ—not the thoughts of the Gospel! If we analyze the beatitudes, for instance, and ask ourselves if our thoughts are Christlike, what will the answer be?

"Blessed are the poor in spirit, for theirs is the kingdom of heaven" (Mt. 5:3). Do we think exactly like this when we lack something?

"Blessed are the meek" (Mt. 5:4). Do we say it perhaps with an irritated heart and tense nerves?

"Blessed are those who suffer..." (Mt. 5:10). Do we really think this way? Do we think just as Jesus?

"Blessed are those who mourn..."(Mt. 5:5). But those who laugh may seem more blessed to us.

"Blessed are you when men reproach you and persecute you, and speaking falsely, say all manner of evil against you, for my sake" (Mt. 5:11). Do we think just like this when someone corrects us?

This Christlike way of thinking depends on the liturgy of the Word. The reading of the Epistle and the Gospel should induce us to think like Christ.

At the close of this first part of the Mass, let us ask the Lord for an increase of faith and the grace of a mind steeped in heavenly wisdom.

Therefore, we will prepare well for the liturgy of the Eucharist, as the instruction on eucharistic worship reminds us: "When the faithful hear the Word of God, they should realize that the wonders it proclaims culminate in the Paschal Mystery, of which the memorial is sacramentally celebrated in the Mass. In this way the faithful will be nourished by the Word of God which they have received and in a spirit of thanksgiving will be led on to a fruitful participation in the mysteries of salvation. Thus the Church is nourished by the bread of life which she finds at the table both of the Word of God and of the Body of Christ."

# The Daily
# Paschal Mystery — 2

Jesus Christ defined Himself as "the Way, the Truth and the Life" (Jn. 14:6). In the liturgy of the word, He is especially our Truth. In the eucharistic liturgy He is especially our Way and our Life.

In the second part of the Mass, the liturgy of the Eucharist, Christ marks out the way for us, which is to follow in His footsteps: "If anyone wishes to come after me, let him...take up his cross and follow me" (Mt. 16:24). Up to what point has Jesus Christ loved the Father? To the point of sacrificing Himself: "Your will be done" (Lk. 22:42). Up to what point has He loved man? To the point of giving Himself completely: "who loved me and gave himself up for me" (Gal. 2:20).

During the liturgy of the Eucharist we should ask the love of God that reserves nothing—that love which brings us to accept fatigue, sorrows, privations and death with the spirit of Christ Jesus.

"By offering the Immaculate Victim," states the *Constitution on the Sacred Liturgy*, "not only through the hands of the priest, but also with him, the faithful should learn also to offer themselves." And the *Constitution on the Church* urges further: "Let all the disciples of Christ, persevering in prayer and praising God (Acts 2:42-47), present themselves as a living sacrifice, holy and pleasing to God (Rom. 12:1)"

In the great Eucharistic Prayer, together with Christ, we give thanks to the Father in the Holy Spirit for all the blessings He gives to us in creation and especially in the Paschal Mystery, and pray to Him for the coming of His kingdom.

The Eucharistic Sacrifice is offered to God, Whose extrinsic glory is increased, by the priest in the name of the Church for the benefit of all. Every need was provided for by our Redeemer on the cross; the same is true on the altars; and the priest offers the divine Victim with the Heart of Jesus Christ Himself.

"In offering this sacrifice," writes Pope Paul in *Mystery of Faith*, "the Church learns to offer herself as a sacrifice for all and applies the single, boundless, redemptive power of the Sacrifice of the Cross for the salvation of the entire world. For every Mass which is cele-

*Our response, "Amen,"*
*at the minor elevation,*
*signifies the total offering*
*of ourselves, our cares,*
*our sorrows, our distresses*
*and our necessities in union*
*with our divine Savior on the cross.*

brated is offered not for the salvation of ourselves alone, but also for that of the whole world."

At the Consecration, Christ is made sacramentally present. The *Mystery of Faith* explains: "In an unbloody representation of the Sacrifice of the Cross and in application of its saving power, in the Sacrifice of the Mass the Lord is immolated when, through the words of consecration, He begins to be present in a sacramental form under the appearances of bread and wine to become the spiritual food of the faithful....

"This Sacrifice, no matter who offers it, be it Peter or Paul, is always the same as that which Christ gave His disciples and which priests now offer: the offering of today is in no way inferior to that which Christ offered, because it is not men who sanctify the offering of today; it is the same Christ who sanctified His own. For just as the words which God spoke are the very same as those which the priest now speaks, so too the oblation is the very same."

It is our privilege to offer ourselves to the Father with Christ our Mediator, the Great Priest and glorified Victim. States the instruction on eucharistic worship: "It is indeed the priest alone, who, acting in the person of

Christ, consecrates the bread and wine, but the role of the faithful in the Eucharist is to recall the passion, resurrection and glorification of the Lord, to give thanks to God, and to offer the immaculate Victim not only through the hands of the priest, but also together with him; and finally, by receiving the Body of the Lord, to perfect that communion with God and among themselves which should be the product of participation in the Sacrifice of the Mass."

After the Consecration, we offer up to the Father Christ sacrificed for our sins, and implore God, in His loving kindness towards men, to be propitious to them, as well as to ourselves and to the dead.

Our response, "Amen," at the minor elevation at the end of the Canon signifies the total offering of ourselves, our cares, our sorrows, our distresses and our necessities in union with our divine Savior on the cross. In Christ let us render adoration, worthy thanksgiving, satisfaction and supplication. Through Him, our Mediator, supreme honor and glory are given to the eternal Father.

The Holy Eucharist presents to us Jesus Christ, immolated for our salvation, from Whom flow in abundance all things good and joyous.

"The Eucharistic Sacrifice is the source and the summit of the whole of the Church's worship and of the Christian life," says the instruction on eucharistic worship. "The faithful participate more fully in this sacrament of thanksgiving, propitiation, petition and praise, not only when they wholeheartedly offer the Sacred Victim, and in It themselves, to the Father with the priest, but also when they receive the same Victim sacramentally."

The Eucharist brings about an intimate union and close friendship between the soul and Jesus Christ: "He who eats my flesh, and drinks my blood, abides in me and I in him" (Jn. 6:57).

The love of God is not idle; when it is present, it accomplishes great things; therefore, not only grace and holiness are bestowed lavishly by this Sacrament, but also one is impelled to action: "The love of Christ impels us" (2 Cor. 5:14).

Thus is realized the exhortation of the instruction on eucharistic worship: "What the faithful have received by faith and sacrament in the celebration of the Eucharist should have its effect on their way of life. They should seek to live joyfully and gratefully by the strength of this heavenly food, sharing in the death and resurrection of the Lord. And so everyone who has participated in the Mass should be 'eager to do good works, to please

God, and to live honestly, devoted to the Church, putting into practice what he has learnt, and growing in piety.' He will seek to fill the world with the Spirit of Christ and 'in all things, in the very midst of human affairs' to become a witness of Christ."

Holy Communion is also a sign of unity, a bond of charity among the faithful. Through Holy Communion we become, member by member, united to the Head, Jesus Christ. "In the Sacrament of the Eucharistic Bread," says the *Constitution on the Church*, "the unity of all believers who form one body in Christ (1. Cor. 10:17) is both expressed and brought about. All men are called to this union with Christ."

As many grains combine to form one loaf of bread and many clusters of grapes unite to produce the eucharistic wine, so we all form but one body in Christ: "that all may be one" (Jn. 17:21).

The *Decree on the Ministry and Life of Priests* declares: the Holy Eucharist "contains the entire spiritual boon of the Church, that is, Christ himself, our Pasch and Living Bread, by the action of the Holy Spirit through his very flesh vital and vitalizing, giving life to men...."

Thus Holy Communion brings about a growth in the spiritual life — strengthening man and perfecting the union of the soul with God: "He who eats me, he also shall live because of me" (Jn. 6:58).

When we assemble for Holy Mass, holy thoughts and dispositions should be cultivated. The Lord Jesus told the Apostles: "Go and prepare" (Lk. 22:8) — go and prepare for the Supper.

Therefore we should come to the Eucharistic Sacrifice recollected in thoughts both sublime and humble — sublime because of the sublimity of this sacred action; humble, because we are aware of our needs.

The instruction on eucharistic worship tells us: "Like the passion of Christ itself, this sacrifice, though offered for all, 'has no effect except in those united to the passion of Christ by faith and charity....To these it brings a greater or less benefit in proportion to their devotion.'"

The Paschal Mystery: passion, death, resurrection and ascension of the Lord, celebrated in the Holy Mass, is to be extended into our life — a life of faith, love and sacrifice.

The Paschal Mystery should permeate our entire life, which is also a mystery of passion, death and resurrection.

We ought to look suffering in the face, to meet it squarely, or at least accept it, giving it the greatest value. One day we will bless it. Thus did the saints, who have suffered and been glorified with Christ, and with them all the souls who journey with fatigue but decision on this earthly pilgrimage to heaven.

St. Paul coined the right phrase to express this truth which can be understood only by people of faith. He tells us that we must suffer together with Christ, and be crucified with Him: "With Christ I am nailed to the cross" (Gal. 2:19). He also tells us that we must die with Him and be buried with Him to resurrect with Him: "If we have died with him, we shall also live with him; if we endure, we shall also reign with him" (2 Tim. 2:11-12).

"We must model our whole life on the life of Christ," Pope Paul said in a sermon which he gave when still a cardinal, "in a union real and *vital*. This is Christianity; this is religion. We must *co-live* with Christ."

"It is no longer I who live, but Christ lives in me," wrote St. Paul (Gal. 2:20). Our lives should not be distinguishable from Jesus Christ in Whom we have been "grafted" according to the Pauline concept; we must form one body with Him, become His mystical body, the whole Christ, as St. Augustine used to say. We must be members of Christ.

"From this stems our dignity, our transfiguration, our redemption, our sanctity and our hope of the future immortal life," continued Cardinal Montini.

The life of Jesus in us, fruit of divine grace and of our correspondence to it, primarily brought about through a loving obedience, is dynamic: it brings us to an ever greater and more perfect love for our Heavenly Father. It induces us to do His will and to seek *His* glory only, always and in everything.

Our entire life is a Mass, to be lived daily and completed only on our deathbed.

And then there will be the vision of God, and participation in the eternal Mass celebrated by the great High Priest, Jesus Christ and assisted at by all the heavenly court.

Declares the *Constitution on the Sacred Liturgy:* "We take part in a foretaste of that heavenly liturgy which is celebrated in the holy city of Jerusalem toward which we journey as pilgrims, where Christ is sitting at the right hand of God...we sing a hymn to the Lord's glory with all the warriors of the heavenly army...we eagerly await the Savior, Our Lord Jesus Christ, until He, our life, shall appear and we too will appear with Him in glory."

Life is one great Mass that will be prolonged in eternity!

# Daughters of St. Paul

IN MASSACHUSETTS
    50 St. Paul's Ave. Jamaica Plain, Boston, MA 02130;
      **617-522-8911; 617-522-0875;**
    172 Tremont Street, Boston, MA 02111; **617-426-5464;**
      **617-426-4230**
IN NEW YORK
    78 Fort Place, Staten Island, NY 10301; **212-447-5071**
    59 East 43rd Street, New York, NY 10017; **212-986-7580**
    7 State Street, New York, NY 10004; **212-447-5071**
    625 East 187th Street, Bronx, NY 10458; **212-584-0440**
    525 Main Street, Buffalo, NY 14203; **716-847-6044**
IN NEW JERSEY
    Hudson Mall — Route 440 and Communipaw Ave.,
      Jersey City, NJ 07304; **201-433-7740**
IN CONNECTICUT
    202 Fairfield Ave., Bridgeport, CT 06604; **203-335-9913**
IN OHIO
    2105 Ontario St. (at Prospect Ave.), Cleveland, OH 44115; **216-621-9427**
    25 E. Eighth Street, Cincinnati, OH 45202; **513-721-4838**
IN PENNSYLVANIA
    1719 Chestnut Street, Philadelphia, PA 19103; **215-568-2638**
IN FLORIDA
    2700 Biscayne Blvd., Miami, FL 33137; **305-573-1618**
IN LOUISIANA
    4403 Veterans Memorial Blvd., Metairie, LA 70002; **504-887-7631;**
      **504-887-0113**
    1800 South Acadian Thruway, P.O. Box 2028, Baton Rouge, LA 70821
      **504-343-4057; 504-343-3814**
IN MISSOURI
    1001 Pine Street (at North 10th), St. Louis, MO 63101; **314-621-0346;**
      **314-231-5522**
IN ILLINOIS
    172 North Michigan Ave., Chicago, IL 60601; **312-346-4228**
IN TEXAS
    114 Main Plaza, San Antonio, TX 78205; **512-224-8101**
IN CALIFORNIA
    1570 Fifth Avenue, San Diego, CA 92101; **714-232-1442**
    46 Geary Street, San Francisco, CA 94108; **415-781-5180**
IN HAWAII
    1143 Bishop Street, Honolulu, HI 96813; **808-521-2731**
IN ALASKA
    750 West 5th Avenue, Anchorage AK 99501; **907-272-8183**
IN CANADA
    3022 Dufferin Street, Toronto 395, Ontario, Canada
IN ENGLAND
    57, Kensington Church Street, London W. 8, England
IN AUSTRALIA
    58 Abbotsford Rd., Homebush, N.S.W., Sydney 2140, Australia